SISTER SECRETS

SISTER SECRETS

A BROTHER'S REVEAL

by Matthew Valan

North Dakota State University Press
Dept. 2360, P.O. Box 6050, Fargo, ND 58108-6050
www.ndsupress.org

North Dakota State University Press
Dept. 2360, P.O. Box 6050, Fargo, ND 58108-6050
www.ndsupress.org

SISTER SECRETS: A Brother's Reveal
By Matthew Valan

© 2018 by North Dakota State University Press
First Edition

Library of Congress Control Number: 2017956371
ISBN: 978-1-946163-04-2

Cover design by Jamie Hohnadel Trosen
Interior design by Deb Tanner
Author photo by Haney's Photography

The events in *Sister Secrets* are portrayed to the best of the author's memory. While all stories in this book are true, some names and identifying details have been changed to protect the privacy of the people involved.

The publication of *Sister Secrets: A Brother's Reveal* is made possible by the generous support of donors to the NDSU Press Fund and the NDSU Press Endowment Fund, and other contributors to NDSU Press.

For copyright permission, please contact Suzzanne Kelley at 701-231-6848 or suzzanne.kelley@ndsu.edu.

David Bertolini, Interim Director
Suzzanne Kelley, Editor in Chief

Publishing Interns: Angela Beaton, Shane Gomes, Zachary Vietz

Printed in Canada

Publisher's Cataloging-In-Publication Data
(Prepared by The Donohue Group, Inc.)

Names: Valan, Matthew, 1954-
Title: Sister secrets : a brother's reveal / by Matthew Valan.
Description: First edition. | Fargo, ND : North Dakota State University
    Press, [2018]
Identifiers: ISBN 9781946163042
Subjects: LCSH: Valan, Matthew, 1954---Family. | Mentally ill--Family
    relationships. | Mentally ill offenders--Psychology. | Adult children
    of dysfunctional families. | Brothers and sisters. | BISAC: BIOGRAPHY &
    AUTOBIOGRAPHY / Personal Memoirs. | SOCIAL SCIENCE / Sociology / Rural.
    | FAMILY & RELATIONSHIPS / Siblings.
Classification: LCC RC455.4.F3 V35 2018 | DDC 616.890092--dc23

SECOND PRINTING

∞ This paper meets the requirements of ANSI/NISO Z39.48-1992
(Permanence of Paper).

To my wife, Kathy, who nearly lost me to the story.
Thanks for waiting.

CONTENTS

PREFACE

All stories, if continued far enough, end in death, and he is no true story teller who would keep that from you.
— Ernest Hemingway, *Death in the Afternoon*

July 22, 2006

She walked slowly yet deliberately through the house and out the kitchen door to the sidewalk, which led to the gravel driveway. She released the lever on the shotgun, and the barrel arched up and away from the trigger mechanism. Her hands, shaking a bit, reached for the shell, which she carefully inserted into the chamber. After she snapped the barrel back in place, she aimed the shotgun to the sky and fired the round. The blast and the kick left her breathless; the explosive power of the weapon stunned her. She paused, bent down, picked up the spent shell casing and placed it in her pocket. With a live round in her hand, she walked robotically into her house, sat down at the kitchen table with the shotgun in her hands, and waited.

CHAPTER 1

"You like to tell stories, don't you?" He asked and I answered,
"Yes, I like to tell stories that are true." Then he asked, "After you
have finished telling your true stories sometime, why don't you
make up a story and the people to go with it? Only then will you
understand what happened and why."
— Norman Maclain, _A River Runs Through It_

This story is true. Telling it helped me understand what happened and why.

November 1979

On a cold, gray November morning the lights of our orange 1948 CJ2A Willys Jeep bounced off the ancient Norway Pines as we drove deep into the woods of northern Minnesota. "God dammit Matt, slow down," my father yelled as he peered out into the pre-dawn darkness. I held back laughter as he bounced up and down on the seat, coming perilously close to being ejected from the open vehicle. We had journeyed down this same trail in a forested area called the Gulch for the past ten years. He brought me here on my first deer hunt when I was fifteen. Hunting trips and ski outings had helped us to bridge the ever widening generation gap which threatened to tear apart fathers and sons in the tumultuous 1970s.

My first rifle was a Remington Woodmaster .308 pump with open sights. I still remember the November day in 1969 when Papa brought me to the local gun shop and let me pick it out. I brought it up to my cheek, pressed the stock tight to my shoulder, and breathed in the scent of gun oil, steel, and wood. I felt like a man. I would carry that rifle into the woods over the next forty deer seasons. Each season would begin with our drive deep into the forest to Tepee Lake. To paraphrase author Norman Maclain: "To my father the highest commandment was to do anything his children wanted to do, especially if it meant going hunting!" The forests, lakes, and mountains became a playground where we sensed the awesome creative genius of God.

Arriving at the end of the trail, we spoke in hushed whispers and sign language. After shouldering our rifles and backpacks, we each walked lightly to the stands where we would wait for deer to move from their evening feeding areas. I stutter stepped down a brush filled draw and up a steep pine ridge to a rock an ancient glacier had conveniently deposited on a high point overlooking a slough we called the Boomerang. This was an ideal spot where my father had shot many deer over the years. He graciously offered me his favorite stand. Papa was that kind of a man, always giving, always looking out for his partner's wellbeing and success. As I prepared for the wait, I placed a four shot clip in my rife and carefully inserted one round into the chamber. A heavy mist collected the sounds and carried them to me from my dad's stand just over a Jack pine ridge. I counted two clicks, one as he slid a shell into the chamber of his .30-06 Remington rifle and another as he inserted the four shot clip. We were locked, loaded, and ready.

Just after sunrise I heard the first shots several ridges to the west of me. I imagined the first deer of the season being killed. A curious sadness followed a rush of anticipation. I recalled my father saying this was a common dilemma for conservation minded hunters. As I pondered his reflections my thoughts were interrupted by the sound of an animal approaching my stand from the well-worn game trail. I held my breath and kept quiet, but it seemed as though my heart was pounding as loud as a bass drum. I raised the rifle up to my shoulder, aiming at the spot where the trail emerged from the buck brush. My index finger rested on the safety. I was ready.

Just as I was wondering what bragging rights for the first deer of the season would feel like, a timber wolf appeared in my rifle sights. It was a magnificent animal, gray with black highlights. I had never seen a wolf before. The wolf seemed as surprised as I was at the sudden face to face encounter. Wolves rarely appear before humans and this fine canine had just found itself facing a hunter. I was aware one of the northland's most legendary hunters had just become the hunted. Although I knew taking a protected timber wolf was illegal, I instinctively clicked off the rifle's safety, took careful aim, and prepared to squeeze the trigger.

As the wolf and I stared each other down, a voice from within asked why I would want to take this animal's life. I was hunting for venison, and I had learned from my father and others one should never kill just for the sake of killing. Yet I struggled with the fact that timber wolves preyed on deer and I was tempted to shoot. In that instant, something deep inside my being prevented me from pulling the trigger. The wolf, however, did not know. The animal appeared resigned to the fact the battle was lost and remained frozen in its tracks, waiting for the inevitable shot to be fired. It was not until I lowered my rifle that the wolf growled and turned, quickly disappearing into the misty depths of the heavy timber.

I contemplated what had just occurred. I thanked God my father had taught me about the sanctity of the hunt, a respect for all of God's creatures, and the value of meeting a wild animal face-to-face in the wilderness without the need to take its life.

Twenty-seven years later a woman would sit at her kitchen table with a weapon locked and loaded. A predator and her prey would come face-to-face and a trigger would be pulled. What happened during that tragic encounter will haunt our family forever. The woman is my sister Cordee. This is a story about Liz and Cordee — my two sisters — born three years apart. Two sisters united in their shared survival of abuse, yet torn asunder by tragic death. It is a true telling about a lifetime of events that conspired to bring Cordee to a sultry July morning when she waited and wondered with her finger on a trigger.

CHAPTER 2

It is those we live with and love and should know who elude us.
— Norman Maclain, *A River Runs Through It*

Awakened from fitful sleep on cold December morning I picked up the phone to hear a nurse calling with news: my father had not long to live. We arrived at the nursing home in time to experience some final moments of clarity before he slipped away. My father thanked me for the friendship we shared, and asked me to care for the remaining loves of his life. Promising him I would care for Mom, his daughter, and the land, which he had entrusted to me, brought him comfort. As death drew near, I laid down in his small bed beside him. Upon feeling his breathing slowing, we sang and prayed familiar prayers. Christmas was two weeks away. I shared the Christmas story from Luke 2 which long ago was committed to memory. It felt as though it came back to me for this very moment. He relaxed hearing the news which the angels shared with the shepherds to "be not afraid." After the birth story, we sang the Christmas carol "Away in a Manger." It was a hymn we had sung together many times during Christmas Eve services at our home church, Hoff Lutheran. Tears came to my eyes thinking this would be the last time we would share it in this life. At the last verse, "And fit us for heaven to live with thee there," my voice found a profound strength. The last notes drifted into his memory, he took a deep breath, exhaled, and then breathed no more. Reaching back for my mother's hand, I experienced instead the gentle embrace of my wife and son. We wept. A husband, father, and grandfather had bravely faced death and he silently flew away into the misty heights of God's wonderful forever.

I knew at the moment of his death I must write this story. Perhaps then I would understand what happened and why.

My father died on December 15, 2010, at eighty-four years of age. Seventy-nine of those years were filled with wonderful experiences including the joys of marriage and family, wonderful friendships, meaningful careers, and an abundance of experiences that would rival most people's bucket lists. His last five years however, were filled with unfathomable suffering inflicted upon him by those he loved most. Much of his suffering emerged in and through his beloved daughters, Elizabeth Anne and Cordee Jo. While he loved them unconditionally, his quest to understand them proved elusive.

He died while still in search of redemption and restoration for his daughters and perhaps even for himself. I wrote in a quest for understanding, seeking a truce with myself and others, attempting to move away from a need for retribution toward the peace of restoring what our family lost.

The two sisters became legends in the minds of many of their contemporaries. Liz and Cordee were beautiful. Both were athletes and campus queens. Young boys and men pursued them, the two sisters finding great sport in the chase, often enjoying the pursuit as much as the catch. They were not averse to titillating and taunting anyone who would agree to play the game. Once while hoeing sugar beets on our farm, they decided to seek tans without bra lines. I was operating a tractor well away from where they were hoeing, but enjoyed watching the startled reactions from those who drove by on the road. One afternoon, two carloads of boys took off from work to swim in the local gravel pit. Speeding off to their break, the lead driver looked out in the field and saw the two sisters with their tanned breasts glistening from Coppertone lotion. The lead driver hit the brakes just as the next carload took note of the view. The vehicles collided and while no one was hurt, the girls always delighted in their ability to stop traffic.

On another summer day when our parents were away from the farm I received a call while working in the shop. As I answered, a panicked Liz pleaded: "Matt, we need your help right away!" Asking her what was up, she simply said, "Drive north on our farm road and after a couple of miles you'll see." It didn't take me long to figure things out. The two sisters had been driving too fast on a gravel road in the Volkswagen Bug our father had given them. They had flipped the car over onto its roof. As I approached I could see the car sitting like a top hat right in the center of the road. I found them at the farm they had called me from, and the two of them were scared shitless. They laughed when I betrayed a smile while trying to give them hell about their actions. We tipped the car right side up, checked the oil, and started it up. They were then off on another adventure. Our parents never learned of the mishap. I protected the two sisters, well aware they had as much information on me as I on them. It developed into a delightful conspiracy of silence that seemed harmless at the time.

We also had an older sister named Kit. She was a child from my mother's first marriage and was off to college in Colorado before Liz and Cordee found their strides. Kit and I shared the blessings and trials of caring for our father and mother as their health began to fail. She came as soon as she could after our father's death. After we embraced and shared our sorrow, Kit walked with her husband Tom to the bed where Papa's body rested. After her time with him we embraced and wept together. It was then Kit shared the story of the day she broke her leg on Big Mountain in Whitefish, Montana. Our father was a member of the first professional ski patrol on the famous ski mountain in northwestern Montana. During the winter of 1960–61, he moved the entire family out to Whitefish where Kit and I attended school. Kit was twelve years old, I was six, and Liz and Cordee were two and six months, respectively. We had planned to ski the mountain on a Saturday after a big dump of snow, and Papa had told Kit to only ski the boot-packed runs. He tried to explain that the off piste areas would be dangerous as the snow was of "leg breaker" type. "Of course I went out there, immediately fell and broke my leg at the boot top." Kit explained. As she continued telling me the story, tender tears fell from her eyes. Looking down on our father's still body for the last time, she turned her head, locked eyes with me intently and said: "I never told anyone this but Papa was the first patrolman to find me on the slope that day. I expected him to yell at me for disobeying him and going off to ski where he had told me not too. To my amazement he didn't. He just kindly went about splinting my break as carefully as possible and calmly told me that everything would be okay. I will never forget his kindness on that day."

For a few more moments we stayed with his body. Suddenly we knew it was time to leave. The memories we shared warmed us, but the body of our father was growing cold. We left the room together, the battles of childhood behind us. We were at peace for a time. However, the wounds from those childhood battles would reopen and the peace would not last.

CHAPTER 3

Too easy to lose the way. Too hard to keep from unraveling when there's nothing to remind you of who you are and where you should be.
　　　　　—Diana Rowland, *Mark of the Demon*

The shotgun was rarely used. It was there for one purpose, which was to dispatch an occasional varmint that might wander into the northern Minnesota farmyard where Cordee's family lived. It rested in a back corner of the house with a box of field load shells within easy reach. I was aware of its existence only because Cordee had mentioned it to me once in a strange conversation. Somehow the shotgun that Cordee purchased at a neighborhood gun shop had remained in the possession of this non-hunting family throughout the years.

　　Cordee was born in the summer of 1960, the last child in our family of four. She was born at the height of the Cold War and in the midst of the sexual revolution. As a child of the sixties and seventies she experienced the cumulative angst and societal upheaval of the age and it impacted her throughout life.

At times I was her protector. Other times I failed her miserably. Because of those failures both perceived and real, I am haunted by what I have done and left undone in my relationship with her.

We were raised in an era and environment where guns were an accepted part of rural life. We were taught to assume guns were always loaded and to check the magazine for shells before handling a weapon. Our father never intended his guns to be used for personal protection. He told us we had the county sherriff's department for that. The guns our family owned were for hunting deer, ducks, pheasants, and an occasional rabbit. We always cleaned and ate what we killed. We learned to know the lethal power of rifles and shotguns. We respected that power. Even though Cordee grew up in the same household where we honored a tradition of hunting, I do not recall her ever handling or firing a gun. Liz, on the other hand, learned to shoot and hunt at an early age. The two sisters shared many interests but never one for guns or hunting. While Liz and I learned early on about the damage a rifle or shotgun could inflict on an animal or target, Cordee never experienced such things. Our baby sister never heard the blast of a shotgun close to her ear or witnessed the lethal power of lead ripping an animal's flesh.

As the youngest of four children, Cordee's early life was a constant dance between overprotection and unbridled freedom. If more checks and balances would have been in place during those formative years her story might have been different. However, as our sister grew into early adulthood we discovered a person much different than the sister we had known earlier. Something inside her was locked and loaded, and the explosive power lay dangerously close to the potential igniters.

Our mother possessed a keen sense of denial and avoidance so we never talked about family issues in much detail. Our father was a boisterous man who often joked around. The sheer power of his personality kept us from honest reflection upon what was occurring in our family. Eventually Cordee's actions conspired to thwart any attempt by either parent to deny or deter her destructive behavior.

If we feel there is no safe place to ask tough questions, to honestly reveal our fears and hurts, the ever increasing weight of the burden becomes overwhelming. Eventually the accumulated hurts contribute to a retaliatory arsenal, which we subconsciously store until our mind calls for help. Each of us has a different tipping point. When, if, and how our individual defense structures release is a continuing mystery locked in the minds of those who contemplate retribution.

CHAPTER 4

I ask not for a larger garden but for finer seeds.
—Russell Herman Conwell, *My Prayer*

Our father was twenty-seven when he got around to choosing a wife. Confirmed bachelors, tied to their mother's apron strings in post-World War II America, faced an uphill battle when it came to courtship. Most of the young women had already been swept off their feet by returning war heroes. Papa was haunted to his dying day by the memory of losing his first love to another man. Yet, when he first laid eyes on our mom her movie star looks trumped all other considerations. He was smitten, and his instant infatuation spawned a half-century love affair. Our father's name was Merlyn, and he was heir to a significant farming operation. Shirlee was a victim of a failed marriage to a traumatized survivor of the epic battle for Iwo Jima. From the beginning, there was an underlying tension in the union. Papa brought to the marriage an intense desire to be loved and needed. Mom brought a need for stability and a four-year-old daughter. Her little girl Kit felt the world changing, but she had no clue as to the quake that would hit when her fifth summer turned to autumn.

My sister watched her mother walk down the aisle in March of 1954, unaware I was developing in secret. I was but a small protrusion protected in our mother's womb, covered by the satin of her wedding gown.

The wedding day spawned a prophetic incident that perhaps alerted the discerning eye as to what lay ahead. After the pastor pronounced them husband and wife, the promises were sealed with a wedding kiss. While the kiss was in process, the daughter of the bride dressed in her flower girl finery, turned and let fly a hard kick to the shin of her mother's new husband. She turned, deftly surveyed the astonished guests, cracked a satisfied grin and sprinted down the church aisle without looking back. Our father remarked years later after retelling the story: "And Kit's been kicking me ever since!"

Born on a sunny October day seven months after the wedding, my incarnation must have been Kit's worst nightmare. I was named with the initials of my grandfather. Christened as M.O. Valan the Third, it was expected I would one day live on and operate the family farm that my grandfather founded in 1903. I felt Kit's disdain and jealousy early on. She often sneered as visiting aunts lovingly called me little M.O. and covered me with kisses. Sibling fighting is expected, but our battles became legendary in the community. Once after tiring from her constant teasing, I reached for the nearest weapon, my father's watch lying on a nearby table. When her taunting became too much, I threw the watch as hard as I could, but she ducked and it smashed our kitchen window. Kit laughed knowing full well I would receive the blame and punishment. Another incident happened when I was older. A fight broke out on the bus while we were riding home from school. I was still small and no match for her much stronger and agile body. When the struggle was over I was left in tears with my new shirt torn off my torso, standing half naked and holding back tears of hurt and embarrassment. Silently muttering the only insult I could recall from my farmyard education, I mouthed, "You bitch." She just laughed and took another swipe at me.

I began to see things more clearly some time later when I was in the heat of an argument with a couple of kids from a neighboring farm. We were in the backseat of our school bus arguing over the merits of Chevys and Fords. Just as I thought I had won the battle, they released their long held secret weapon. "Oh yeah," the pencil-necked kid stuttered. "Kit is only your half-sister! Your dad isn't her dad!" Shocked and awed I sat in silence, intuitively knowing what they had said was true. I had been publicly shamed by my family's conspiracy of silence and denial. The new information was confirmed after my "say it isn't so" plea was greeted by silence at our family's table that night. When my parents had planned to tell me what the entire world already knew, I could only imagine.

Kit went away to college in the fall of 1965. I was eleven, Liz seven, and Cordee five. Kit was extremely bright, but the temptations of Denver, Colorado, in the sixties overwhelmed her. The world she was so adept at controlling soon controlled her. After being kicked out of college she landed in San Francisco. Haight Ashbury, the Grateful Dead, and a slick East Coast boy running from a prominent Jewish family changed her life forever. In the charismatic young man she met her match. The next time she returned to Minnesota it was with him and she was pregnant with his child.

As the gossip travelled around the township, our parents whispered privately in our farmhouse on the windswept Red River Valley prairie. Our overbearing father and silent, brooding mother tried in vain to control the uncontrollable. One morning in 1969, I awakened to find my future brother-in-law sleeping on the floor across the hall from my room. He was wrapped in a multi-colored Indian-print blanket. His massive bush of curly jet-black hair was the only part of him I could see. I had encountered my first hippie.

I was not the only one whose world was being rocked. My father and mother had been invited guests at President Nixon's inaugural ball just months before. They were the perfect GOP couple, and my father was being considered as a congressional candidate. At breakfast that morning I silently looked on as my parents struggled to grasp the changes swirling through our family. The world as they knew it was ending. The generational clash of the sixties was playing out in our little farm kitchen over Corn Flakes and scrambled eggs.

I had heard whispers about shotgun weddings but never imagined one would actually occur in my living room. The two hippies played along. Allen looked like a college Republican with his massive bush of hair gone, shorn well above his ears. Kit looked more like a prom queen than an acid queen, and everyone pretended all was well. The conservative Lutheran pastor did his duty with sufficient grace and after a few poems, prayers, and promises, the loose knot was tied. Before we knew it they were on their way back east, accompanied by my sister's new in-laws. A new life had been arranged with a job for him in the family business and societal expectations for Kit.

The two of them returned to Minnesota a few years later and established a cult following. The cult was an extension of The Way International, and it caused damage to Cordee and her friends. The Way identified charismatic men, recruited them, and trained them to establish youth groups in small communities with a system that trashed traditional Christian beliefs and practices. The leaders identified popular and impressionable high school students, training and using them to bring in their friends. The process eventually pulled teens from their churches and caused deep rifts in families. They called themselves "the saints" and were taught that everyone on the outside was suspect. Cordee was a popular homecoming queen and track star with many friends; her popularity was used to grow the group. Drugs were eventually introduced to Cordee and her friends. Cordee recalls Kit's husband kissing her and passing cocaine from his tongue to hers. By introducing Cordee to drugs, he maintained control over her and perhaps many other teenaged kids. Eventually Kit's husband tired of the Midwest, the ministry, and Kit. The marriage dissolved and Kit recanted everything the cult stood for, saying she had found the "true biblical Jesus." The kids from the cult, who had grown into young women, were told to burn their Way materials and find the "true faith." The results were devastating to Cordee and many of the others. A number of those young women eventually underwent psychiatric care and continued to struggle for years afterward.

CHAPTER 5

Well, it has been said that there is no grief like the grief which does not speak.

— Henry Wadsworth Longfellow, _Hyperion_

From the time I can remember he was part of our lives. He was the first full-time hired hand on our farm after my father and my Uncle Orlen dissolved their partnership. The two brothers were not destined to be partners in anything. The only thing ever holding them together was my grandmother, who held title to 1,400 acres of prime Red River Valley land. Once the land was received from their mother, the boys were free to strike out on their own.

The two sons marched to very different drummers. Born to a detached father in his sixties, the boys were raised by a grace-filled but overprotective mother. Orlen, the younger of the two, had a steel-trap mind and an innate gift for farming. Through a series of bad decisions, he steadily traded a bright future for dark barrooms and loose women. Sold out by the local bank, he surrendered to drink and a hurtful divorce followed. Orlen had a good heart, but as he soaked it in gin and whiskey he became a bitter and lost man. My father became co-dependent, and our entire family went awash in the toxic situation nearly drowning in the flood of cover-ups and explanations. Bad choices made because of an alcoholic personality would impact our family for years and indirectly contribute to the accumulation of tragedies that loomed on the horizon.

I sometimes wonder what two healthy, sober, and faithful brothers could have achieved with the assets they had at their disposal. I will never know. I do know every action causes a re-action, and we would feel the effects of illness and moral failures for the balance of our family's history.

As my father struck out on his own, his first task was to find a hired man to help him work the eight-hundred-acre farm. Dave, the new hire, was big and strong. He was a high school dropout who chain smoked and occasionally drank himself stupid on weekends. He stayed a few yards from our farmhouse in a small, one room bunkhouse. He washed in our basement mud-room and relieved himself in an outhouse behind our shop. My father trusted him implicitly. Every morning we would find him slumped in the corner of our tiny farm kitchen waiting for my mother to serve him breakfast. He took most of his meals with us, often arriving at the table before my mother emerged from her bedroom. Dave held ugly cigarettes in stubby fingers emerging from fat hands connected to tree-trunk-sized arms that were supported by elbows planted firmly on the table. His beady eyes squinted tightly as he inhaled the toxic smoke into his lungs and exhaled the remaining fumes into our tiny, vulnerable respiratory systems. Little did we know that for the two sisters a room full of smoke would prove to be the least of their problems.

These days I am an ordained pastor trained to recognize sexual predators. I am proud to say I have helped scores of abused children find help and justice. However, as a pre-teen Midwestern farm boy with my own issues, I was ignorant of the warning signs.

The hired man would always arrive from the bunkhouse early, and his punctuality earned him the respect of my father. His dastardly diligence was rewarded with cheap thrills as my night-gown-clad sisters ran down the stairs from their bedrooms to our only bathroom. His corner seat at the kitchen table afforded him an unobstructed view as they walked down the hallway.

Papa and I stood by as all of this happened. I was too young to know better, and my father, eager to please, wanted to believe everyone deserved his trust. If my father would have known what his associate was scheming, he would have castrated him on the spot. Instead, he would go to his death thinking the hired man was worthy of his trust.

Some details of the hired man's crime are lost in the retelling, because his actions became known many years after the incident. The two sisters were asleep in an upstairs bedroom. Cordee was awakened by the sound of heavy steps on the stairway. The old hardwood floors creaked as the monster approached the room where the two sisters were napping. Entrusted to watch the children for a short time while our mother was away, he seized his opportunity to appease his twisted desire. By the time Liz awoke he was near the bed. The two sisters caught a scent in the room of stale beer, cigarettes, and grease. Paralyzed with fear but instinctively knowing she must protect her younger sister, Liz rolled over onto Cordee while feigning sleep. By doing this she came between the hired man's searching hands and Cordee's tiny body. As the little girls remained still, his stubby, tobacco-stained fingers reached under Liz's panties and violated her fragile vagina. While Liz endured the penetrating pain alone, both sisters would carry the pain deep inside themselves for a lifetime. Cordee would never forget the sacrifice Liz made for her, and it would bind them together as sisters in arms. An enduring alliance of sisterhood was born.

The 1960s was a decade when our country faced massive changes. However, those changes came slower to farm communities. Fears were often faced and endured in silence. It was a time of trust, and if that trust was violated an oft-used coping mechanism was to embrace denial. It was a time when finding the courage to explain what scared us or what we felt, eluded us. That time is past, buried in history. However, even that which is long buried is sometimes exhumed, and the resurrected monsters continue to stalk the victims as painful memories surface.

Recently I had a discussion with a female cousin of mine. After asking the details of Liz's abuse my cousin's face turned ashen and she grew silent. "When I was six years old that hired man did the same to me. He didn't penetrate me but touched me under my panties and masturbated as I laid in fear. I've never told anyone until now." For fifty-seven years my dear cousin bore that grief alone, thinking somehow she was to blame

I do not remember when or why, but one summer the farmhand did not return and the bunkhouse remained empty. He was the last hired man to live on our farm. We did not grieve his leaving. I grieve over what we did not know, over the grief the two sisters and my cousin silently endured alone.

CHAPTER 6

My make-up wasn't smeared, I wasn't disheveled, I never finished off a bottle, so how could I be an alcoholic?
— Betty Ford, *Glad Awakening* (with Chris Chase)

It was late August in the summer of 1976, and the heat in downtown Kansas City, Missouri, felt like a blast furnace. I walked from my downtown hotel room to Kemper Arena with a Minnesota smile on my face as wide as Lake Superior. I had come to Kansas City as a student intern on President Gerald Ford's campaign staff, and after working hard all week in the trenches I finally had a ticket to the GOP convention. I was on my way to the evening session. It was to be the night in which the party would nominate its candidate for the November election. President Ford and former California Governor Ronald Reagan were locked in a tight contest for the nomination and the nation was buzzing. One of my fellow interns happened to be Marcy Rumsfeld, the daughter of the Secretary of Defense. She had invited me to join her and her family in the presidential box for the historic evening. For a political science and history major from a small Midwestern private college, this was pretty heady stuff.

Expecting to remain in my basement cubicle during the convention, I had only packed jeans, t-shirts, and jerseys for my trip. I can still remember the look on the face of Donald Rumsfeld. He was the Secretary of Defense and sixth in the line of presidential succession. He appeared irritated as his daughter introduced him to her fellow intern from Minnesota who was wearing blue jeans and a 1977 Concordia College football jersey. To this day I can't believe he allowed me to join his family on one of the most important nights of his political life. His now famous scowl is still locked in my memory. Marcy, a bit of a rebel, seemed to get a kick out of introducing me to the rest of her family, former Texas Governor John Connelly, and finally to Betty Ford, the wife of the thirty-eighth president of the United States of America. Mrs. Ford extended her hand and greeted me warmly and, as she did so, I noticed she appeared to be under the influence of some substance. Her eyes were glassy, and when she welcomed me, she gestured like she was directing a large choir. As the first speaker was introduced, I took my seat with the Rumsfeld family just two rows behind Mrs. Ford, her family, and their guest, Tony Orlando, a popular singer of the time. A stifling tension competed with my excitement of being so close to people of such power and popularity.

At that time my father was a politician at the state level in Minnesota and also served the president on a national agriculture board. As the son of a political figure, I had seen the lost look on wives and children not unlike what I was observing in the presidential box. Public service takes its toll on families at all levels.

Betty Ford and Nancy Reagan faced each other from their boxes on opposite sides of the arena. When Mrs. Ford was introduced, Nancy Reagan clapped politely. When Nancy Reagan was introduced and the band played a verse from "California Here I Come," Betty Ford stole the spotlight by dancing an aggressive jig with Tony Orlando. I watched from behind as Jack and Susan Ford hid their faces from the glare of the national television cameras while their mother carried on in front of millions of viewers worldwide.

Years later Betty Ford went public with her addiction. She established the Betty Ford Treatment Center, which has helped thousands of women deal with their addiction issues, many caused by the men in their lives. Betty Ford died in July of 2011. The world remembers her as a woman of admirable courage.

I have learned that men are able to inflict suffering on the women in their lives in different ways. For centuries women and children have lived in the shadows of men who spent time away in pursuit of fame and power. Our family would not be immune to the pain ambition inflicts. My mother, along with Liz and Cordee, would bear the brunt of my father's absence.

I left Kansas City and that fall married Kathy, the love of my life. I remembered what I observed on that hot August night at the convention. For forty-one years I have tried to be a present and supportive spouse and an engaged parent to our three children. Our family shares an amazing wealth of love, but it is something that takes time and tending. Years ago we buried the myth that quality time is all that is needed to foster healthy relationships. The source of quality time is quantity time, and we work diligently to achieve it.

By the autumn of 1976 my mother and my two sisters needed help, but family pride, public image, and denial made getting help nearly impossible. The cost of inaction would be enormous.

CHAPTER 7

When a man assumes a public trust, he must consider himself public property.
     —B. L. Rayner, _The Life of Thomas Jefferson_

We celebrated my father's hard-fought political victory in the fall of 1978. After two recounts he was declared the victor, and in early 1979 he became a member of the Minnesota House of Representatives. If only one could count the cost of certain endeavors before they commence; in retrospect, our family paid an overwhelming price for the service Representative Merlyn Valan rendered to the people of Minnesota. When a hired man crept into his daughter's room, Merlyn was serving as Chief Clerk of the State Senate. When the two sisters were in their formative years, their father was spending weekdays from January to May two hundred thirty miles away at the state capital in St. Paul. By the time he retired as Assistant Commissioner of Agriculture for the State of Minnesota, his accumulated debts were overwhelming, and he needed to sell farm land. The public trust extracted a heavy toll during the time my father was public property.

The two sisters danced between the freedoms granted them by our emotionally overwhelmed and image-conscience mother and the suffocating control that our father tried in vain to manage from a distance. The dance was both delightfully intoxicating and madly sobering. It was a dance that ultimately brought excruciating pain to all involved. Along the way, however, we fell in love with the dancers, and that love blinded us to the damage done. Once, when Liz was in junior high school, she took advantage of some time alone. Liz put on one of our mother's wigs, propped up two pillows on the seat of the '69 Camaro, and made plans to drive to town and meet her girlfriends. Before she left the farm, she went out to the barn, took one of my weanling 4-H project pigs, wrapped it in a blanket, and set it in the passenger seat. A thirteen-year-old girl driving a Super Sport Chevy with a pig riding shotgun! It was a delightful stunt everyone in town knew about except my parents and me.

Our father was a good man who hovered around the edges of greatness. Like many men who just missed the fighting of World War II, he lived in the shadows of those who went off to save the world from tyranny. He countered a constant struggle with self-esteem by creating a loud and overbearing persona, which was seen as loveable by some and boorish by others. His public service was one way in which he quenched his immense emotional needs, emotional needs that evolved from a vacuum created by a proud elderly father who enjoyed the center he occupied in the family system. My father had to have it both ways. He loved and cared for us, yet he needed more than our family could give him. Public service became an addiction, and the lure of our state and nation's capitols took him away when he was needed most.

I played on the high school football team in the early 1970s. In those days, teams celebrated an event called Dad's Night. Before kickoff, all the fathers would line up on the fifty-yard line, and as our names and numbers were called we would run up to our fathers, hang a cardboard cutout of our number around their neck, and shake hands. It was my junior year, and I was disappointed when my father informed me he needed to be in Washington for political business on the night of the event. He suggested I call my Uncle Orlen to fill in for him. My uncle said he would be glad to do it, but when I showed up to remind him, I discovered him passed out drunk in front of his television. I experienced the impact of two men suffering from addictions on that night. Perhaps one was more respected than the other, but the end result was a disappointed son and nephew.

One day I was called out of class to take a call from my mother. It was the first time I had heard her cry. She called to tell me our garage was burning. My father was away on political business and Mom was left to bear the burden alone. He came home to the farm as soon as he could, but the stress of the event clearly had a devastating effect on my mom. She desperately needed her husband to lean on rather than her adolescent son.

As I think back on my father's career in public service, I do so with mixed feelings. I know he served his state and nation faithfully and with distinction, but I am also keenly aware of the many costs our family endured during his absences. I was too young to fill the void my father left, and I needed more guidance and support in those formative years.

My father's political service spanned fifty years. The emotional and financial costs to our family were overwhelming and had a direct impact on the health and wellbeing of us all. In the end it would prove to be more than we could bear.

Papa compensated for his absences in many ways. We enjoyed snow skiing in the winter and water sports in the summer. We were loved by our parents and embraced by extended family and good neighbors. Faith was valued. We attended church regularly and prayed at family meals. We ate well, wore clean clothes, and lived in an ample farmhouse built by my grandfather in 1950. Horses, dogs, and cats roamed the farm, and we were free to play

from sunup to sundown. Life appeared to be good and in many
ways it was. However, the effects of absence, abuse, denial, pride,
and unrestraint were beginning to take a silent toll on our family.

CHAPTER 8

You can't kill the spirit, it's like a mountain old and strong;
it lives on and on.
— Naomi Littlebear, *Like a Mountain*

Our mother was born on the windswept prairies of west central Canada. Her mother was the daughter of a successful wheat farmer. Our mother's father was a hard man, a braggart and blowhard who beat his three girls and their mother as well. Unable to make anything for himself in Canada, he took his wife from the good life on her father's farm to a hard life in Minnesota. Although she bore him three wonderful girls, he never forgave her for not producing a son.

My mother was deeply affected by the actions of her father. Late in life I showed Mom a photo of her young father next to a fine dog. The image burned into my mother's dementia fogged mind. "Oh yes," she said, "I remember that dog. Dad treated it better than us. He was a mean man." More than mean, my grandfather was heartless. Shortly after the family moved from Canada, his wife was injured in a skating accident. She required surgery to correct the injury, but the doctor made a terrible mistake, leaving the young mother paralyzed from the waist down. My grandfather abandoned her and the three girls, without providing any financial support. With three young girls to clothe and feed, there was no other choice than for my disabled grandmother to go on welfare. With nowhere to turn she became a fundamentalist Christian who looked with hope to the faith healers roaming the land. Later, in loving kindness, my mother's sister Norma and her husband Norman invited my grandmother to live with their family. Norman was a fine man who made up for the shortcomings and moral failures of my grandfather. Norman walked my mother down the aisle on the day she married my father. Her father chose not to attend the wedding.

My mother would never forget the shame that resulted from her father's sins. Feeling the pain and hopelessness of poverty, she focused on the one asset she possessed. Her beauty was perfect in the post war years. Dark alluring eyes, long dark hair, lush lips, and a classic figure would help her escape from poverty. Beauty was her most valued asset, a gift she was born with. Along with her natural beauty and sheer perseverance she emerged from poverty and abuse and made a life beyond her wildest dreams.

Before Mom died in December of 2014, I would walk with her down the halls of the nursing home where she resided. I sensed her attempt to return to the woman she once was. I noticed familiar side glances to see who might be looking. I watched her flirt with the guys as some long hidden survival mechanism kicked in. I wept for her and all she had lost. Yet, occasionally I caught a gleam in her eye and a bounce in her step and I sensed for a moment she had returned to another time. I remembered those times as well when she wore elegant evening gowns, a mink stole, or the latest ski wear. For one brief shining moment she was dancing at a Governor's Ball, skiing down Dollar Mountain at Sun Valley, or traveling across Europe. The moment quickly faded as her face turned toward mine with an expression reflecting fear and confusion.

CHAPTER 9

*The battle to keep up appearances unnecessarily, the mask —
whatever name you give creeping perfectionism — robs us of
our energies*
          —Robin Worthington, *Thinking about Marriage*

My father always liked fast cars. Even as an old man, one-legged
and enduring terrible pain, he would amaze me by noticing hot
cars pulled up beside us. "Jesus! That's a good looking machine,"
he would say enthusiastically. "Who makes that?"

His love for cars would bring us great joy and even greater
pain. One of the first cars I remember driving was a super-charged
Chevy Corvair. The rear engine Corvairs were a cousin to the
Corvette, just as fast but easier to flip. Our family learned to love
speed. My dad also loved the look on my mom's face when he
brought her home a new sports car. It seems he could never quite
find the right coat or dress, as she would nearly always return
those gifts. However, he always scored on his car choices. After
the Corvair, he bought her a sweet, cherry red, 1966 Chevy Mali-
bu convertible, and she loved that car. When he brought it home,
she was forty years old and at the top of her game. Her jet-black

hair, sleek figure, and signature black and red clothes matched her new red sports car perfectly. Always aware of image, she was taking modeling classes and took pride in being a Cheri Paul model from Fargo. It might have taken awhile, but my mom's dream of marrying young and retiring finally happened when she got the attention of a Red River Valley farmer. Life was good.

Once, while filling out a form for school, Mom corrected my response under family occupation. I had written "farmer," and she reminded me our occupation was not simply farming but rather sugar beet growing. Ah, planters rather than simple farmers. Mom loved the lifestyle, which included grower banquets, presidential balls, dance clubs, dinners, and mixing with the rich and famous. She golfed and skied regularly along with maintaining an aggressive travel schedule.

In the midst of it all, I felt loved. Each day my dresser drawers were magically filled, my bed made, and the house always clean. I rarely waited long for her to pick me up after an event, and it was great getting picked up in those sweet cars. She was a great mom.

When the cream Camaro convertible with orange stripes and hound's-tooth interior pulled into the farmyard, we were ecstatic. The 1969 Super Sport was the Indy pace car that year. Those cars were the signature car of the sixties. Our mother was sharp, and she turned heads when she drove it. She joyfully let me take it out a lot and I had tons of fun in it. Once on a lake country road I was taking corners way too fast, all four tires skidding through the blind curves. Roaring out of a curve with increasing speed I was shocked to encounter people crossing the roadway going from one beach to another. Hitting the brakes and swerving caused the car to hit loose gravel and careen out of control. Parents and children were running, some diving away from the car's path. At the last possible moment the car found an opening between the road, water, and pedestrians. It was a miracle no one was hurt. Scared and guilt-ridden, I just kept on driving. My sisters were not the only ones who behaved recklessly in those years.

We eventually traded the Camaro for a pickup, which probably saved my life. However, Papa kept up the gift giving by buying Mom a 1977 yellow Pontiac Grand Prix for her fiftieth birthday. It was the last car Mom really liked. She protested loudly when Papa started buying Buick Park Avenues, which she called old people cars.

I mention the fast cars and my behavior because an image was created that my two sisters struggled to keep up all of their lives. The girls measured success in all the wrong ways. Success for them was not education, altruism, or even faith, but rather appearance. Glittering images of tanned bodies, the latest fashions, good looks, and sleek, fast cars defined how my sisters saw themselves. Misplaced priorities not only contributed to a number of car accidents throughout the years, but also led to an accumulation of at-risk behaviors that compromised our family's financial future and brought about tragic outcomes for all involved.

With our father's political schedule growing more intense in the 1970s and '80s, my mom was left to ride herd on her daughters. Liz graduated from high school and was sampling colleges, tempting boys, and indulging in alcohol and weed while attempting to manage wide personality swings. Cordee was known as sweet and fun-loving, a track athlete who was elected high school Homecoming Queen. Everyone loved Cordee. She had a warm, inviting personality and played guitar and sang like the folk rock artists of the time. Yet, we began to see subtle changes in our beloved Cordee. Her involvement in the aforementioned Way International created a rift between her and our family, as well as coaches and teachers. This scary fundamentalist cult turned Cordee and her friends away from their families and messed with their minds. Our sister Kit and her husband Allen were at the center. They drew the kids into a convoluted, drug-fueled hysteria, a disaster that distanced Cordee from those of us who could have helped her.

All these things happened while our father was attending to the public good. The two sisters were running wild with too much freedom, money, and low expectations. Our mother tried to reign them in but was in over her head. She was an uneducated victim of abuse who did not understand the importance of higher education. She valued image over substance and it was a recipe for disaster. In fact, mini-disasters were occurring regularly and breaking the family apart. At the same time the mental health of my mother, father, and two sisters was beginning to erode.

CHAPTER 10

How easy it is for a heart to turn to stone.
—Mary Morris, *The Halls of Meteorites*

Many problems can be averted if we receive adequate warning and take action. Our mental state is not as predictable; our minds are wonderfully and tragically complex. Looking back over our family's history, I am aware of our dysfunctions. Yet even as I reflect on the pain, much of it could have been avoided. Perhaps this is why I feel such a need to share our story, even at the considerable risk of causing more pain to the family. While it is true our family has endured more than its share of pain, we have embraced the pain, endured the struggles, and moved on to live happy and productive lives. All of us except the two sisters. Liz is dead. Her ashes lie buried a few miles south of the farm. Liz died on the Fourth of July in the summer of her forty-seventh year. She died while struggling to be a good mother to her three children, birthed from the seed of two men whom she tried yet failed to love completely.

A few days before she died, Liz was in Texas fighting an ex-husband for the custody of her two children. I traveled to the small Texas town to support her uphill battle. It is often advantageous in war to fight battles on familiar terrain near necessary supply lines. She fought her battle on southern ground far from her support systems. She fought and lost in her ex-husband's home town, in a court ruled by a judge who called her children's father by a home-boy nickname. Tommy had a benign enough little-boy name, but he was a ruthless manipulator who went after my sister's emotional jugular, branding Liz an unfit mother. Liz maintained her composure during the hearing even as the opposing attorney impugned everything about her abilities as a mother. This was the final salvo in a battle between Tommy and Liz since he had aggressively pursued and lured her away from her husband in New Mexico. Liz and her first husband, Joe, had only been married a couple of years. Joe, an English graduate from the University of Minnesota and a gifted writer, lived with Liz in a rustic cabin near Angel Fire, New Mexico. They were working on carving out an adventurous life in the mountains with their son. My wife, our daughter, and I were visiting them for the weekend. Liz and Joe's marriage was vulnerable, and unbeknownst to us, Liz and Tommy had plans. She left on her own volition, hearing a call beyond her motherly instincts. I would not believe it if I had not been there to observe her flight. It came without warning as we were bathing our toddler children, laughing as the two little cousins frolicked together in the tub. Liz said she was going into the laundry to fetch a towel. She never returned. I called to Joe and Kathy in the next room. They responded, "Isn't she with you?" Just like that, my sister was gone into the cold winter night. No excuse, no explanation.

What possessed her to leave just then? How could she not postpone her carnal desire for another night or at least until the end of the bath? Liz had to have been experiencing deep pain at multiple levels. Perhaps the genesis of her moral and emotional breakdown emerged from that moment she rolled over to protect Cordee from the assault of the hired man. The abuse spawned a deep-seated insecurity and negative self-image, which grew as she watched that monster take his seat at the family breakfast table every morning for many years. While we may never truly know why, we do know that the consequences from that frigid New Mexico night led to a divorce. She eventually married the man she snuck away to meet. It was a damn shame she left a good man for a poser who called her Lizzie with his soft Texas drawl. I never understood her actions. I liked and respected Joe, still do in fact. He tried his damnedest to love my sister.

While I will never understand why Liz did what she did, I do know that when my sister called, I dropped everything and made the long trip to Texas to defend her honor in that dusty hamlet where Tommy had lived in his youth. She didn't have a chance in his home territory. With the drop of the gavel, she lost her children.

Two longtime girlfriends traveled to Texas to support Liz. Her dear friend Gust also made the trip. Their support meant so much to my sister. Their presence was a lifeline for her.

Licking our wounds, we made our way north to Minnesota, along with Liz's children. The judge had granted Liz her request to have a week with the kids before they moved away to be with their father. Unknowingly, Liz was embarking on her last trip with her kids and spending the last days on earth as their mom. We could not know that in forty-eight hours my beloved sister would be dead. Her death would set into motion events that would change all of our lives forever.

CHAPTER 11

Every living thing is a survivor on a kind of emergency bivouac.
—Annie Dillard, *Pilgrim at Tinker Creek*

Our son was ecstatic to have his two cousins visiting the farm over the Fourth of July holiday. He was enjoying the summer between his seventh- and eighth-grade years, but the farm could get lonely at times. Our son was the youngest of our three children, and his older sisters were often away with their friends. He was oblivious to the stress his Aunt Liz had experienced in Texas, and he loved her fun, spontaneous spirit. Liz loved her children and, when healthy, she was always seeking out fun activities for them. This particular holiday was even more special because she had a short week with her kids before they would be whisked away by their father. Flush with his custody victory, Tommy was already planning to move them far away from Liz. Liz was on a timer, and she was aware how fast it was ticking.

Since Liz was a young girl, she had suffered long bouts of depression followed by short intense bouts of manic energy. On the morning of July 4, 2005, Liz was shifting into high gear, fueled by energy pills, caffeine, and the presence of her children. Our father had a cozy relationship with his long-time physician. He had a supply of Hydrocodone pain killers for an old shoulder injury and ample Ritalin pills for narcolepsy. I am now aware she would steal my father's pills whenever she had the chance.

My heart still aches when I think back to the pain my sister was experiencing during that fateful week. The public humiliation she endured in that Texas courthouse, mixed with the angst of giving up her beloved children to a man she despised and who physically abused her, was unbearable. Liz was doing her best not to let her worries show. She arranged to spend the day and early evening at a good friend's lake cabin forty miles east of our farm. The day promised to be filled with swimming, jet skiing, water skiing, and cruising on the pontoon. It was just the kind of Fourth of July we had experienced as kids. A day of outrageous family fun! I cannot help but think Liz hoped a great day together on a Minnesota lake might help her children change their minds regarding living arrangements.

Our youngest child ran up to his mom and excitedly asked if he could spend the day with Aunt Liz and his cousins. "Please, Mom, can I go?" he said to Kathy. Upon sensing her apprehension he turned to me with pleading eyes, "Please, Papa, it will be so much fun. I haven't seen my cousins for so long . . ."

Kathy and I exchanged one of those classic glances honed from years of parenting where snap decisions are made without verbal consultation. A pregnant pause confirmed our mutual concern as coded messages developed over twenty-nine years screamed a silent *no*. However, sympathy trumped common sense, and we found ourselves nodding *yes*. It was a nod we would come to regret.

There are few days in my life for which I would request a do-over. The shoulda, woulda, coulda moments of my journey pale compared to the times I have sat with my loved ones and thanked God for the blessings. I am a man who exudes optimism, and I nearly always find the good in any situation.

However, July 4, 2005, takes first place on my short list of regret filled days.

My forty-seven-year-old sister Liz still bore remnants of her youthful beauty. She was crowned Snow Queen in college and skated as a hockey cheerleader during high school. I have a picture in my memory of her almond eyes highlighted by her naturally olive-colored skin and the long dark hair that fell on her shoulders as she buckled the kids into her SUV. I will always cherish seeing her joy as the three children jumped into their seats with an enthusiasm that makes one recall the endless summer days of youth. We waved them off from the farmhouse. Kathy and I, along with my parents, watched from the lawn, silently harboring our private concerns. Liz had sorely tested our trust before, and now — with our eyes wide open and those concerns concealed by cautious smiles — we uttered private prayers. Even our most guarded thoughts gave no hint that one of those leaving would never come home to us.

Sympathetic concern and altruistic actions can turn to anger and guilt in a moment. Kathy and I were asleep in our cabin after a day of riding horseback in the national grasslands just west of our farm. Liz's refusal to leave the lake at our agreed time had left us angry. Sleep eventually came but not before our parental guilt marinated for a long time.

Our cell phone calls to Liz had been going nowhere so eventually we gave up. Liz would do as she damned well pleased. As usual, her logic was driving us crazy. We knew she had to be home for her midnight nursing shift at the local hospital. As the minutes ticked by we calculated the miles she had to cover and the time she had to do it. She was running out of time. We knew her penchant for speeding. When we factored in heavy holiday traffic on curvy, lake country roads, our worst fears made sleep fitful.

Kathy and I were awakened by the harsh ring of our bedside phone. As pastors, we know a late night ringing phone usually signals a crisis. Our thirty years in professional ministry had prepared us to respond with the clarity of fire fighters. However, on this night we would not be called to respond to the needs of our congregational flock. Instead, we would draw on every skill, every prayer, and every emotional reserve we possessed as we were thrust into a crisis of epic proportions. The voice on the other end of the line was the Texas ex.

"There has been an accident," he said in his Texas drawl. "The information is not totally clear but the people on the scene believe there is a fatality. Three others are being transported to Detroit Lakes by ambulance; one may have life threatening injuries." My veins pushed ice as I tried to clear my mind to make sense of what I was hearing. I struggled to breathe.

There had been a rollover. Liz's daughter had managed to get a call through to her father on a rescue worker's cell phone. For the moment, the Texas ex was an ally. We were united by our concern, grief, and hope. For a moment it was genuine, but the unity would not last. As Kathy and I fumbled blindly for our clothes we found our minds spinning with the possible outcomes. In the midst of the confusion, we took a moment to embrace and pray. Twenty-nine years of marriage had taught us to depend on prayer when our world was spinning out of control. Crying, I prayed for God to give us the strength to endure what we would face in the hours and days to come. Our spoken prayers retreated inward. We continued the frantic pace of preparation, which included constant attempts to navigate the emergency dispatch systems for information. All we could do was to hope and pray our son was alive, being protected and sustained by skilled first responders.

When my call finally got through, the state trooper's voice was painfully measured. He told us the fatality was an adult woman whose body was being transported to the county morgue in Fergus Falls. He went on to say three juveniles, one with serious injuries, were in route to a Detroit Lakes hospital. How does one rejoice as a father and grieve as a brother? How do a mother and father pray the injured child is not their son while knowing it might be a niece or a nephew? I looked across the pasture and trees that grew between my parents' farmhouse and our log cabin. I could see my father and mother were up, waiting anxiously for their daughter and grandchildren to return. Liz was overdue. After several heated conversations, she had finally called to alert them she had left the lake. "Drive safely," our father had pleaded. In her hyper anxious state, Liz may have heard his words, but he had no power over whether she would heed them.

Before we could depart from the farm to cover the fifty-five miles to the hospital, I would have to stop and tell my dear mother and father their beloved daughter was dead. Some tasks in life are impossible to escape. I gathered my father and mother in my arms and told them as gently as possible that Liz had been killed in a rollover not long after she had left the lake. "The children," I said with all the tenderness and hope I could muster, "are alive." It was clear Papa did not hear anything else beyond the unbelievable news Liz was dead.

He fell to his knees weeping uncontrollably. This strong man had been drained of all his strength. In his brokenness he was inconsolable, utterly unable to reach out to his wife of fifty years who was standing next to him, lost in a cloud of dementia. We had no other option but to leave them alone in the house they had shared since their wedding day. The blessings of the old house still outweighed the curses, but blessings land lightly like a sweet kiss while curses hit harsh and heavy as a punch. This curse would prove to be the precursor to another. We could not know the events of this night would one day cause a devastating tear in the fabric of our family. A heavy curse would be revealed just thirteen months in the future. The countdown would begin as soon as the news reached Pennsylvania.

Kathy and I are at our best alone. We share a love for the ages. Our love was built on the solid rock of a mutual faith in

God. When situations or people get between our faith and our love, any evil gets leveled and pulverized with only good emerging. This is not a Pollyanna-like untested love. We have faced death, poverty, and loss together. We have emerged from life's challenges stronger and more solidly in love. On that tragic July Fourth evening, we would need each other's support more than ever before.

The drive was long and all we could do was silently pray while pondering what realities we would encounter. As we drove into the unknown, all we had was our love for each other and a shared faith in a God whom we knew loved us and the children. Fate, however, had taken a child from us through Sudden Infant Death Syndrome twenty-three years earlier. We could not imagine facing such grief again. We claimed the promise that God would protect our dear son. It was all we had to hold onto.

I cannot imagine another moment which will bring the relief we felt as we ran into the emergency room and saw our precious son alive. Prayers of pleading turned to prayers of thanksgiving as we learned his injuries were not life threatening. We wept in each other's arms.

CHAPTER 12

*In a real dark night of the soul it is always three o'clock in
the morning*
      —F. Scott Fitzgerald, *The Crack-Up*

I will never forget the unbridled joy I experienced as Kathy and I
embraced our son. I had made a mistake that nearly cost his life.
I did this knowing my sister was living on the edge, burdened by
immense stress. By allowing sympathy to trump common sense,
we threw our son into this danger. He came within inches of not
surviving it.

I was aware my parents and Liz's children would bear the
brute force of the grief. Cordee would also be deeply affected,
more so than anyone could imagine. Together we spent hours
trying to make sense of it all. Grief is complicated when anger,
guilt, relief, and joy collide at the intersection of family losses.

After the funeral we gathered at the crash site. We painstak-
ingly walked the road from where she first entered the turn to the
ditch where the vehicle finally came to rest. After confirming she
had not been drinking, we wondered what other factors might
have contributed to the crash. She had only been driving a few

minutes and we all knew Liz usually drove wide-eyed and hyper during her emotional highs. Although the children had drifted off to sleep, it was highly unlikely Liz would have dozed off in such a short time. Speed certainly could have contributed to the crash; Liz almost never drove the posted speed limit. It was also possible a deer or a raccoon could have caused her to swerve and lose control, but she was a good enough driver to negotiate the curve. There had to be something else.

I returned to the site many times and drove the curve alone at high speeds without any problems. After each trip to the crash site, I would sit with my grief-stricken father who was trying desperately to make sense of it all, asking question after painful question. The answers eluded us time and time again.

The epiphany hit me like a blinding flash of light. It came as Papa was sharing with me the final cell phone conversations he had with Liz on the night of the accident. I too had called Liz urging her to head for the farm, but I had given up in frustration and gone to sleep. Papa had persisted, calling her every few minutes until the conversation between father and daughter became tense. He told me his last call was never answered. This news penetrated my brain, and I immediately took the conversation in another direction. I am not sure if I succeeded in taking him off the scent. I suspect I will never truly know if he saw the shock in my eyes. If he did, he would conceal it until the day he died. Indeed, it was the last call he made to his beloved daughter. I believe as she reached into her purse to pick up her phone to argue with him once again, her front tire hit the roadside gravel and her vehicle began to slide.

The *if onlys* continue to haunt me. If only Liz would have received partial custody in that Texas courtroom. As a result of the judge's decision, she felt pressured to deliver a perfect day and night for her children. She pushed herself beyond her physical and mental limits. If only she had ignored the cell phone ringing incessantly from the dark recesses of her purse and not taken her eyes off the road for that fateful moment. Yes, the *if onlys* continue to haunt me, because maybe one of those situations could have been altered enough to keep the Trail Blazer from going off the highway and into a tragic roll on that humid summer night.

Our son only remembers his Aunt Liz's scream and then silence. Her scream commenced as the tires bent against the resistance of the cooling pavement. The compressed energy released and sent the SUV high into the air, slamming it back to the ground and crushing the vehicle and her body on impact. The car rolled several times. The children survived the crash because they were belted in and small in stature. Liz remained strong at the wheel, fighting with everything she had to bring the careening vehicle under control. Once the car went airborne all hope was lost. Elizabeth Anne Valan would not survive the wreck.

Our son regained consciousness in a roadside ditch, the darkness penetrated by flashing lights. He looked up into the face of a rescue worker from where he lay after his cousin had kicked the car door open and pulled him from the wreckage.

To know why or how something has happened sometimes brings peace. As Norman Maclean wrote, "it's one of the most beautiful poems in the world: now we know."

My father died not knowing why. I may not ever know either, but the quest itself has brought me peace. One thing haunts me. Perhaps the man Liz had depended on most during this wild and tumultuous time had unknowingly contributed to her death. God rest our dear father's soul.

CHAPTER 13

*What stays with you latest and deepest? Of curious panics,
of hard fought engagements or sieges tremendous . . . what
deepest remains?*
— Walt Whitman, *The Wound Dresser*

We gathered on a splendid sun-splashed day to bury Liz's ashes in the dark prairie loam, which covered the bones of our paternal ancestors. The heavy, grief-filled days of July had yielded to the cooling breezes of early autumn, and our collective family soul embraced the respite. We dug the hole together, each sibling taking a turn, boot to steel, steel to sod, until a grave took shape. With the spade firmly in hand, our father listened as the pastor spoke the time-honored words of the Christian committal rite: "It is in certain hope of the resurrection of our Lord Jesus Christ that we commend our sister Liz to the Lord and commit her body to the ground, earth to earth, ashes to ashes, dust to dust." I heard gentle weeping as I knelt to the ground and laid the urn in place. The shovel made another round through our family as each of us sprinkled soil over the remains of our sister. Finally, our father tenderly tapped at the loose accumulation of dirt as if he were tucking Liz into her eternal sleep. After a time of silence, he looked deeply into our eyes and through profound grief pleaded for us to take care of each other and be safe.

The earthly bond between the two sisters was severed, and it became painfully clear Cordee was devastated. They were best friends, but within the friendship Liz had emerged as Cordee's protector. I was oblivious to it growing up. I have learned I was raised very differently from my sisters. While I was the beloved only son, the girls found it necessary to forge an alliance to cope with our mother. Our mother was very loving, but her love included an inherent need to manipulate a few precious aspects of her life.

From early morning until bedtime her small kitchen was her command post. Like a sentry she maintained her position, armed with strong coffee and smoking Pall Mall straights. With the wall-mounted Bell telephone at her right, the kitchen sink behind her, and the pantry to her left, she was able to withstand any frontal or flank assault. It was the place where she met the myriad joys and sorrows of her life for over fifty years. It was the sanctuary she retreated to when her unspoken questions outnumbered her answers. While other kitchens served as teaching centers and places of bonding for mothers and daughters, Mom's evolved into a one-person cockpit. As the years rolled by the rigors of stress and age cruelly stole her beauty and mind, but her kitchen corner retained its familiarity and enveloped her like a trusted friend. When we began to notice she was forgetting essential ingredients in familiar recipes and neglecting to pay overdue bills, her beloved kitchen corner became a bunker to shield her from the gathering storms of dementia. By the summer of 2005, however, no bunker would be strong enough to shield her from what lay ahead.

The sadness which remains is the fact that two sisters never enjoyed the wonder of standing on chairs with sleeves rolled up and tossing flour to and fro with their mother. It was more often a place to be shooed away from. It was a place of loving production rather than loving mentoring. Ironically, what was produced in that corner from our mother's loving hands contributed to a joyful kitchen table, one with shared conversing and good-natured teasing. Meals began with a prayer, and many wonderful family celebrations occurred around our table. Neighbors were greeted, grandbabies cuddled, words of blessing spoken, and it was good. However, one by one we moved away only to be reunited during holiday gatherings or vacation reunions. Our connection to home, like for most adult children, had changed. Yet change was hard for Liz and Cordee to accept. Liz and Cordee drifted in a confused state of perpetual adolescence brought on by abuse, illness, and an absence of accountability.

The two sisters shared more than natural beauty and a zest for life. While Cordee is the only family member who carries a bipolar diagnosis, Liz also apparently suffered from the disease. The condition is treatable under the care of a physician along with a careful mix of medication, diet, exercise, and honest friendships. If any of these are absent, however, the effects can be debilitating. Without the dreadful disease the two sisters could have effectively danced their way through the complexities of life. However, the extended periods of depression with the accompanying tedium and flat, hollow banality only served to exacerbate the accumulated stresses they encountered. Conversely, their mania continued to fuel appetites that could only be satisfied with destructive behavior.

Our family could never find a way to honestly talk about the struggles each of us faced. My heart broke as Cordee finally found the courage to share the story of the abuse Liz endured at the hands of the hired man. The conversation occurred as the two of us were driving to a family gathering a few days following Liz's burial service. So much of what I had previously struggled to understand about Liz and her erratic behavior suddenly made sense. After the truth-telling, I wandered through the secret spaces of my mind, finding corners I had previously avoided. The denials which I detested in my parents and siblings became painfully real as my wanderings continued. Our farm had several old buildings that my grandfather had constructed in the early 1900s for storing grain, machinery, and for sheltering livestock. By the 1960s some of the structures had fallen into disrepair while others had been repurposed. The old summer kitchen and an accompanying ice storage house had originally been built to feed the farm crews, which seasonally numbered one hundred men during harvest and planting. As farming practices changed and our family began raising sugar beets, the buildings were moved to a far corner of our farmstead and used to provide summer housing for the families who came from Texas each summer to weed the beet fields. As many as five families would live on our farm for the entire summer and into early fall. Each family had as many as six children ranging from infancy to upper teens. My sisters and I experienced a multi-cultural lifestyle as those children became our summer playmates.

As Cordee was sharing the story of the abuse Liz endured, I found myself remembering being led into a dark, dusty wheat storage building by one of the migrant boys who was a few years older than me. I was eight years old. Liz was four and Cordee not yet two. Kit was a teenager, honing her anger and teasing skills on a regular basis. I was thankful to have a friend and the older boy was eager to influence me in many ways. Some of those ways were fun and full of adventure while others were wrong. The fun celebrated inclusion and the joy of sharing in a vibrant Tex-Mex culture. However, the shame of the wrong retreated and became locked into the recesses of my mind for years. When Cordee revealed Liz's secret, I was instantly back climbing the ladder to that secluded grain bin in the back of the storage building. The older boy had promised a day of shooting sparrows with our home-made slingshots. What actually occurred came back to me in a painful memory as Cordee and I drove into the night, deep in conversation, our eyes staring straight ahead at the road. From that moment on I came to more fully understand my dear little sisters. I weep for the little boy who could not say no to the older boy who pulled his pants down and tried to violate him. I weep for those little girls who dared not say no and run from the house yelling for help. As my sisters and I endured the abuse and shame, no one was there to dry our tears no one heard our cries. At least Cordee and Liz had each other to lean upon. However, after Liz's car came to rest, crushed and upside down in that muddy Ottertail County ditch, Cordee was left to bear her burdens alone.

CHAPTER 14

Beneath those stars is a universe of gliding monsters.
—Herman Melville, *Moby-Dick*

One day the monsters gliding through Cordee's head began to take control of her actions. I was driving down a busy avenue near the West Acres Regional Shopping center in Fargo, North Dakota. In a metro area of over 100,000 people it was not uncommon to encounter strange people doing crazy things. Off in the distance in the middle of the busy road, I saw a woman gesticulating wildly and wearing a long flowing gown. Noticing that drivers were swerving to keep from hitting her, I approached slowly and carefully. I could barely believe my eyes as I watched the woman approach cars and beckon them seductively with curved fingers and mouthed expressions. "That's Cordee!" I blurted out to Kathy. "What the hell is she doing?"

Acting on impulse, brotherly love, and embarrassment, I pulled over in heavy traffic. After getting out of my 1979 Chevy Blazer, I called her name. She looked at me with an expression that was a curious mix of the hunter and the hunted. It was a terrifyingly seductive challenge in her piercing, flat gaze that haunts me to this day. In an instant she sprinted away.

At twenty-six and in fair shape, I could still cover one hundred meters in decent time. I needed every second to catch my sister who was a strong middle distance runner. As she hit full stride I reached her and threw her over my shoulders like a sack of wheat seed. While I wrestled her into the back seat of our SUV, she was hurling X-rated expletives at me and clawing at my eyes. This was my introduction to my sister's highly charged and crazed manic state. I had been a high school and college wrestler. I put her in an arm and head lock and instructed Kathy to drive to the local hospital. In those days it was possible for a family member to put a three-day hold on an individual who was deemed dangerous. My parents made the difficult but necessary decision to commit her. Cordee was diagnosed with bipolar disorder and what followed were the awful pendulum swings. Normalcy was fleeting and agonizingly elusive.

While Liz had endured unexplainable highs and lows for most of her life, Cordee's behavior was remarkably stable through high school. She points to a decision made following a year of study at a Folk High School in Norway as the trigger of her pattern of unexplainable behavior. She had promised Grandmother Anne she would save her virginity until marriage. Cordee took great pride in the keeping of that promise. Upon her return from Norway however, she made the decision to give up her virginity to her longtime boyfriend as his birthday present. Overcome by guilt and sensing a new sexual awakening, she found herself spinning in a wash of unbridled sexual need. After a number of sexual liaisons, which included a drug-fueled tour with a local punk rock band and seducing a longtime family friend, she felt her mind rapidly shifting gears from super low to overdrive.

Once, after an extended hospitalization, she was on the run in a hyper manic state. After being asked by my parents to help track her down, I discovered she had forged a check on our father's account. She managed to convince the bank tellers her father wanted her to withdraw $900.00 in cash. Her winsome and trusting Homecoming Queen smile trumped their concerns. With the cooperation of the one airline in our city I accessed the list of those who had flown within the time she had disappeared. Nothing seemed to stand out amongst the typical Midwestern names until the manifest revealed the name G. Sportivo. It looked suspicious and with some sleuthing we soon learned Cordee had flown to California. In a couple of days, she finally phoned after waking up in a group hostel and discovering all of her cash had been stolen by her new friends. Broke, alone, and on the low end of her bipolar swing, G. Sportivo, a name she had lifted from a music album, was back to being Cordee and needing our help. I named our next cat Sportivo just for grins, and the story made for many laughs throughout the years. When it came to the two sisters and their antics, we often chose laughter over tears. The tears would come soon enough.

We all struggled as a family to come to grips with this wonderful young woman's struggle with mental illness. We, along with many others, loved her. In our small farming community we were simply not equipped to cope with the long spells of zombie-like behavior and the short blasts of manic activity. In a relatively short period of time, she washed out of two very expensive private Christian colleges. Our parents were overwhelmed in their loving and diligent efforts to help her, and they often turned to me for advice.

I was of the sophomoric opinion that the medical establishment was taking the easy and irresponsible way out by overly medicating Cordee. We turned to the National Outdoor Leadership School in Lander, Wyoming, with the hope an extended wilderness sojourn might help. The trip out west, however, convinced my wife and me that Cordee was indeed very sick and needed more help than fourteen days in the mountains could provide. Although the rigors of wilderness survival and the clear mountain air seemed to revive her for a time, she could not escape the "gliding monsters" that trolled her mental universe. After returning to Clay County, she once again spun out and landed in the psyche ward of our local hospital. It was there she would meet the man who would become her husband.

CHAPTER 15

On the breast of her gown, in Red Cloth, surrounded with an elaborate embroidery and fantastic flourishing of gold-thread appeared the letter A.
—Nathaniel Hawthorne, *The Scarlet Letter*

One could not ignore Cordee's beauty or resist the sensuous allure she possessed during her manic highs. She had a lovely voice and played guitar and sang splendidly. Even during her lows there was a somber, reflective allure that caused men to contemplate the mysteries hidden by the disease. The dreaded bipolar diagnosis not only tempered but also piqued the desire in men who were drawn to her. It hung over her like a scarlet letter at a time when the disease was still often called manic depression. Steve Tungseth could not resist the inner beauty and raw talent that occasionally broke through the storm clouds encasing Cordee. He was six years older than Cordee. A recovering alcoholic, he had fathered a child with his first wife and was working as an aide on the mental health unit where Cordee had been committed. He too wore an invisible scarlet letter. Steve was the son of a conservative Lutheran pastor. He had distanced himself from his family's strict religious code since his rebellious high school years. He was the typical designated "wild ass" of a pastor's family, and he seemed to relish the role and claim it for himself. Steve was a very strong man with a rangy, roughhewn physique. His piercing eyes and sharp tongue could sting or bless, and he used his words and physical presence to bring order to his universe. Rumors persisted that in his drinking days he was mean, hard, and ruthless.

Cordee, who was raised with a strong father figure, fell hard for Steve, and he for her. Breaking all established protocol, Steve pursued this patient who used her seductive powers effectively. By the time she was released, a serious relationship had evolved. Steve and Cordee met shortly after Cordee was admitted to the hospital. As she was waiting to be assigned a room, Steve walked into the holding area, smiled at her, and held out a pack of Kent cigarettes. She picked one and he lit it for her with his lighter. As she smoked, they visited. Steve was an aide on the unit and Cordee ultimately became one of the patients he was responsible for. During her stay in the hospital, which lasted several months, Cordee and Steve developed a strong attraction for one another. Steve, ignoring specific boundary rules, allowed the relationship to continue. After a couple of months Cordee was granted day passes to go to the public library, but she would lie about her destination and stop by his apartment, which was located just a few blocks from the library. Cordee, still under a doctor's care and heavily medicated, met with Steve several times a week over a span of months. Cordee rode her blue and white bike from the hospital, past the library, to Steve's apartment where they had sexual intercourse regularly.

After Cordee's release from the hospital, their sexual relationship continued, and Cordee became pregnant. Steve pressured Cordee to marry him, but she was confused and unsure. During this time Cordee and Liz talked at length about what Cordee should do. Liz agreed with Cordee that marriage to Steve just didn't feel right. Even back then Steve was controlling and demanding, and Cordee wasn't sure she wanted those attributes in a life partner. Intuitively they may have felt Steve had acted against hospital rules and accepted standards, but they never imagined that what he had done may have been a crime. Nevertheless, Cordee, with Liz's support and against Steve's strong opinion, decided to have an abortion. Liz accompanied Cordee to Minneapolis, and helped to arrange and pay for the procedure. It was during this time Cordee learned that Liz had also had an abortion during high school. The secrets the sisters shared — beginning with the abuse by the hired hand — had accumulated over the years. Pain, physical and emotional, drew them closer than ever. They shared secrets no others would know for years.

Steve continued to pursue Cordee even as she tried to develop relationships with other men. She could not resist his continuous stalking. Sexual needs overpowered her common sense and in a few short months Cordee again became pregnant. This time she was feeling trapped while at the same time enjoying her time together with Steve. She finally consented to marry him. No one except Steve, Cordee, and Liz knew of the unethical actions perpetrated upon Cordee by Steve as she was a vulnerable adult under his care.

However, like her mother thirty years before, she knew her biological clock was ticking, and there was something that drew her back time and time again to Steve. He was handsome, strong, and loved to live on the edge. Against the advice of her sister Liz and ignoring a voice from deep within her being, Cordee said yes to Steve's pleading and demanding proposal. Their baby was growing inside of Cordee; the wedding plans were made in haste.

The little country church was dressed in the liturgical colors of ordinary time. The bride was extraordinarily resplendent, aglow with a hope destined to spring eternal on that June day. Cordee pleaded to have a wedding dance, but Steve said no. He demanded it be a simple affair and that is what it was. Cordee, who was used to the extravagance of her father, received her first glimpse of the different life she would experience with Steve.

My parents and I had no knowledge of Steve's violation of Cordee's rights as a patient. We were ignorant of the abortion and Steve's incessant demands to have Cordee marry him. Ironically, we felt a strong man would be good for Cordee. We let our fatigue cloud our judgement or at the very least hold back our questions. In fact, the marriage helped calm our fears for Cordee. Although the illness continued to pursue her, we trusted Steve knew full well what he was getting into, and we were glad to be getting a respite from being responsible for her.

Their marriage evolved into an itinerant routine as Steve chased construction jobs from St. Paul, Minnesota, to the Red River Valley where Cordee had been raised. A few months after the wedding their first child was born. The family appeared happy, but it was clear Cordee was still overly attached to the Valan home farm. Steve, on the other hand secretly wished his wife would reflect the core values of his mother and commit totally to him. Even though they had heard the words of Jesus read from the red-lettered Bible at their wedding ceremony, the man clearly had not left his mother, and the woman had not left her home.

A semblance of normalcy settled around the family as a second daughter was born. Cordee and Steve purchased a farmstead in Pennsylvania that was surrounded by good friends they had made in the local church. A good job in New York City allowed the family to live a lifestyle previously unheard of, and soon twin boys were born. Cordee was not suited for her mother's chosen profession of homemaking. From a distance she appeared to be overwhelmed with the care of four young children and a husband whose work days were long and hard. The solid core group of friends from her church and an understanding pastor helped keep Cordee centered for a time. However, she always felt that her disease and sin left her exposed in the close-knit faith community, where law often trumped the grace the church of her youth championed. She was caught in the middle, and her prior experience in the Way added to her confusion. Sometimes her mind would wander to a faraway place where Cordee would imagine her protector, Liz—far away in Texas—fighting the same battles of the mind and silently suffering from the same disease. Cordee would fantasize whisking away to Europe with Liz, unencumbered by husbands and family, free as they had been in their youth.

CHAPTER 16

_____

Caresses, expressions of one sort or another, are necessary to the life of the affections as leaves are to the life of a tree. If they are wholly restrained love will die at the roots.
—Nathaniel Hawthorne, *The American Notebooks*

Steve worked excruciatingly long days, rising early for the long commute to the heart of New York City. He loved the vibe of New York. Its ethnic diversity and classic eastern in-your-face conversation contrasted with the passive-aggressive "Minnesota-Nice" he grew up around. It has been said absence makes the heart grow fonder. However, a troubling extension of the familiar saying is absence makes the heart grow fonder for one who is near. Affairs between Cordee and random men had plagued the marriage for years. Just the way Cordee wrapped her lips around a cigarette could send strong sexual invitations to men who were looking for adventure. When these men came on to her, she often welcomed them.

Steve did his best to hold things together as the family navigated the turbulent waters of Cordee's disease, but as the reports of sexual infidelity mounted, he responded with threats of leaving and taking the kids with him. Steve understood, however, that the logistics of working and caring for the family alone would be more than he could handle. With seemingly no options, a very tenuous situation simmered and occasionally boiled-over due to Cordee's instability and Steve's refusal to nurture her insatiable desires. Being a man of sexual appetite as well, Steve continued to have sex with Cordee. The sex was raw and hard, but a disturbing practice emerged in their lovemaking. Steve began to hold back kisses as a way to punish Cordee for her sexual wanderings.

As time went on, Cordee began to yearn for the intimacy sexual intercourse could not fulfill. She craved the affectionate kiss, and soon this obsession became the goal of her extramarital dalliances. In the midst of the tension, their oldest daughter extricated herself from the family drama and enrolled in a Lutheran boarding school in Minnesota. Fatigued by filling in for an emotionally distant mother and a work-strained father, she found a future and hope in Fergus Falls, Minnesota.

Steve and Cordee had dreamed about moving back to Minnesota for years, but good friends, a solid faith community, and a great job kept them from leaving. It took an act of terrorism to set into motion the move that would ultimately bring the family to a pastoral farm on the banks of the Pelican River.

Steve had witnessed the first bombing of the World Trade Center and had a nagging feeling New York City was becoming increasingly unsafe. On September 11, 2001, when the planes hit he was working in a building just across the street. Looking out the windows, he saw people fall to their death, their expressions ranging from resignation to terror. Those visions, mingled with the sounds of bodies hitting the pavement, merged with images of his wife falling into bed with other men, haunting him.

There are solid, time-honored protocols that prevent hospital staff members from developing relationships with patients. Somehow, that restriction did not prevent Steve from pursuing Cordee. From the moment of their first meeting, when Cordee was most vulnerable, the seeds of potential abuse were sown. Steve had unlimited access to her records and witnessed her moments of weakness. During their dating and marriage there were times when it seemed as though he had a choke collar around her neck. When he barked his orders it was as if a leash were being pulled, always reminding her of who held the keys to the locked ward. He knew more about her than a boyfriend should. She never received the fresh start that patients hospitalized for mental illness need and deserve.

Cordee and Steve tried desperately to love one another. At times, they succeeded, such as during their spectacular camping honeymoon into the Boundary Waters Canoe Area of northern Minnesota. But Cordee, who was used to travel and lavish gifts from her father, soon discovered her pragmatic and frugal husband had little time for such foolishness. Although they shared seasons of love, by the time they planned their move back to Minnesota in 2005, the calm seasons had ceased. Steve and Cordee had entered the winter of their life together, and the storms raged.

When Cordee and Steve left the East Coast, they left behind a supportive community and relative prosperity. The placid, conservative aura of the Midwest held the promise of a safe haven and a new start, but the safety they sought would depend on a woman who was coming undone. Cordee was awash in confusion, forgetting how to be a wife and a mother.

Upon arrival in Minnesota, Cordee was deeply grieving the death of her sister, the shock and sting of the tragic loss still fresh. While her stoic husband delivered as a material provider and regular lover, he was devoid of romance, true intimacy, and understanding. She continued to crave his kisses and loving caresses, but he seemed bent on punishing her in their lovemaking. Cordee attempted tender, understanding conversations. Those conversations often turned into lectures from Steve.

Her irresponsible spending habits and long periods away from home continued to take a toll on the relationship. Exasperated, Steve pursued other interests at the expense of helping Cordee seek out the help she needed to cope with the loss of a sister and the spin of the disease.

From time to time she would treat herself to gifts of lotions, scents, or linens. More often than not, he would order her to return them to the store unopened. His stern voice and hurtful gaze would send her off to an internal refuge of her own making. For Cordee, solace was quiet intimacy. She tenaciously sought out what Steve was denying her. All she wanted from Steve were soft touches, tender kisses, and understanding. In the end she tired of asking. Other men would offer what Steve failed to provide. Cordee was not equipped to reign in the desires she stirred up in herself or in the men who pursued her.

Like a loaded firearm, emotions eventually trigger a release of energy. Sometimes the release is harmless. Other times, however, the release propels harmful energy into a situation. Cordee and Steve's emotions were on the brink, highly charged and armed.

While it was a gift for Cordee to escape the temptations of the East Coast, the great loss was leaving her friends who served as witnesses and confessors. She left emotional baggage in Pennsylvania, but the move back to the Midwest would mean facing the emotional demons of her past. She was moving back to the land that had birthed her sickness. She was reentering the land where she had been abused.

CHAPTER 17

A hurtful act is the transference to others of the degradation which we feel ourselves.
—Simone Weil, *Gravity and Grace*

The little farmstead had all the possibilities for a fresh start. The old dairy farm with the peaceful river running through it had the potential to be a place of blessing rather than curse. As always, though, much of life depends on our choices, and healthy choices often depend on healthy minds.

Cordee and Steve were desperately attempting to choose life. However, so much of the past and present was conspiring against them. Looking back, one is tempted to blame parents, siblings, friends, enemies, and perhaps even religious traditions or organizations. One could second guess pastors, doctors, and other professionals. We could even point to the salesperson who sold Cordee the shotgun or the system that allowed it. In the end, though, it has to be acknowledged a terrible disease was the origin for everything going so horribly wrong. All else aligned in a terrible conspiracy of timing. Cordee and Steve made choices resulting in outcomes they never intended. Others made choices along the way that compromised the integrity of the relationship, ultimately leading to its tragic end.

Following the move to Minnesota, positive healthy choices buoyed the family, and a short season of happiness prevailed. With the kids enrolled at a small private Lutheran academy and with supportive friends and family near, Cordee and Steve maintained a peaceful coexistence for a time. However, the season was short lived as external forces converged to impact Cordee's emotional state. A point of no return was approaching.

Moving to Minnesota meant a change in psychiatrists for Cordee. A change in medication levels and the loss of a physician's familiarity and trust sent her into a spin. These changes, along with Steve's inability to find work to support the family as before, brought increased stress into the relationship. Steve was forced to drive long hours following low paying construction jobs in faraway towns. With the children working jobs and involved in summer activities, Cordee was left alone for long periods with limited responsibilities and less money. Soon the credit cards were maxed out, and Steve's anger justifiably flared. While he never laid a hand on her in anger, he also neglected to lay hands on her in a loving way. She soon sought intimacy elsewhere. Much to her surprise, Steve began to hint he may do the same.

We do not know exactly what happened, but looking back it's apparent Cordee and Steve went to war with each other shortly after arriving in Minnesota. They began by choosing their weapons. At first the weapons were icy stares and extended silence. Cordee's stares were hollow and void of any emotional connection. It was scary when she fell into these trances because she had the natural ability to let her light shine in such a kind and gentle way. She would regularly exude a spirit of compassion and gentleness. Steve's intense, iron stare could melt her trusting warmth away, sending her into fight or flight mode. More often than not she would flee and seek understanding elsewhere. Her actions would infuriate Steve. He used every strategy to restrain from raising an abusive hand. He did, however, by his very countenance, have the ability to inflict terror in my sister, draining her fragile self-esteem. He used this strategy knowing full well what he was doing. Steve was at the end of his rope, struggling to find solutions to a family crisis that was escalating rapidly.

For the first time in their marriage, talk of divorce began. Legal papers had been prepared. Cordee knew Steve's first marriage ended in divorce over anger and control issues. Not one to seek counseling, he was on the verge of physically wrestling Cordee into line. The couple was running out of options. Cordee was on a manic high resulting in unprecedented irresponsibility and unaccountability. A toxic mix of fear, grief, desire, and jealously was sending her on a downward spin. And, another man whom she thought loved her was simply leading her on.

In former times of madness, Cordee always knew she could count on Liz. Cordee still reached out to Liz often by visiting the windswept cemetery where her ashes lay buried. Not long after Cordee moved back to Minnesota she was seen by a neighbor lying prostrate on Liz's grave trying to assuage her grief and perhaps asking Liz what to do next.

The two sisters, twisted together in life, had been torn asunder by death. Cordee had survived past crises because of the comforting and protective alliance she shared with Liz. Cordee believed Liz's death occurred in part because of the stress and misery she was enduring in Texas. Together they shared a fear of the men they married. After Liz's death, Cordee bore the fear alone. Without Liz, Cordee reached out to our father who had always been the rock in her life. But in the summer of 2006, he was of no help to her. After he collapsed in my arms on the night Liz died, his health went on a rapid, downhill slide. When Cordee needed him most, he was lying in a hospital bed recovering from the loss of a leg due to advanced arterial disease. One day she visited him in intensive care after she had come from a beauty makeover session. She had not eaten in several days. Overly made up and with hair extensions, she was hardly recognizable and looked like a cross between a super model and a call girl. I wondered how Steve would react. I got my answer when I saw her the next day, with no visible signs of the drastic make over. Steve was bearing down. He'd had enough.

Our mother could not help either. She was fighting her own battle against advancing Alzheimer's disease and, without her husband's help, she could no longer live independently. By the time Cordee was in her most desperate straits, the house our mother moved into as a new bride sat empty on the prairie. The kitchen she had controlled like a Navy Commander's Bridge was still and quiet. The place Cordee knew as a refuge no longer existed, her last escape option closed. In her troubled mind, she could imagine only one place to turn.

CHAPTER 18

Where are the loves that we have loved before when once we are alone and shut the door?
      —Willa Cather, _L'Envoi_

He was our father's friend and Cordee's last romance. He was bright, influential, and knew better. A portly, shaggy sort, one would not imagine him as a romantic. My sister clearly saw something in him besides wealth. Cordee knew he had dated our two sisters. Nevertheless, she welcomed his advances and met him in secret. She fantasized he would somehow be her ticket out of her troubled marriage. He gave her the intimate affection that Steve withheld. Whether he inferred it or not, she believed she could run away with him and start a new life. Long phone conversations led to arranged meetings. The meetings led to embraces, which led to the tender kissing Cordee had longed for over the years. While I sat alone tending to our very sick father, she was seeking romance in secret. I think Steve knew what I did not. Cordee's makeover and long hair extensions were not for him but for another man: one who was deceiving a husband and a father who called him a friend.

Sensing something was going on, and enraged by this latest dalliance in a long pattern of infidelity, Steve retaliated by going to see an old girlfriend. Unlike Cordee, Steve made no attempt to hide his actions. Rather, he told Cordee exactly what he had done and added that he planned to see her again. It has been said hell hath no fury like a women scorned. Cordee proved the truth of this in her response to Steve's liaison. He knowingly exacerbated the situation when he told Cordee he may, in fact, be drawn to kiss the woman. Cordee became insanely jealous. Inexplicably blind to her own adulterous actions, she focused only on her husband kissing another woman.

The vagaries of Cordee's disease blurred her capacity to make sense of the fantasy world she imagined, drifting between the mania and the depression. Delusional, Cordee believed it perfectly acceptable to be planning secret rendezvous with other men while experiencing rage over the thought of Steve doing the same thing with another woman. As the heated argument evolved into a fight, Steve boldly proclaimed that because Cordee had sought out other men, he would do whatever he wanted to do with whomever he pleased. Cordee retaliated by stating her astonishment that Steve would give another woman what he had steadfastly denied her. For his part, Steve had decided he could no longer live with the fact that Cordee was brazenly giving herself to other men. In retrospect the solution seems relatively simple: Steve wanted Cordee to be faithful; Cordee longed for the romance of his kiss. Neither, however, could deliver the empathetic love they both so desperately sought.

On the evening of July 21, 2006, an eerie silence hovered over Cordee and Steve's white frame farmhouse. From the entryway, if one listened carefully, the calming waters of the Pelican River could be heard washing over the rocks. Steve broke the silence with a question about Cordee's unexplained absences. She responded with disrespect and he raised a hairbrush, an act she interpreted as threatening. The brush never made contact, but it was the first move in a domestic battle. The battle quickly escalated turning the placid evening into a turbulent storm of angry threats and icy stares. Later, barging into the bathroom unannounced, Steve yelled at Cordee and took a swing at her. He made contact with her toothbrush, knocking it from her mouth, spattering toothpaste on the mirror. No direct eye contact was made, but Steve's reflection in the mirror inflicted terror in Cordee. They retreated to different areas in the house. Ultimately sleep came for them both, but it was fitful, filled with toxic thoughts and dark dreams.

On the morning of July 22, the emerging heat of the day could not melt the glacial ice that had encased the marriage. Nevertheless, Steve made his traditional pancake breakfast for the children before sending them off to their summer jobs and activities. Later, as was his custom on days off, Steve walked to his Harley Davidson motorcycle, started the engine, and drove down the farm drive to the open road, seeking solace, freedom, and perhaps some answers to cope with his wife's ever changing mental state. As he was leaving, the sound of the big Harley engine drifted over the bed where Cordee was napping, the noise stirring her from sleep. It would be the last time she would awaken as a free woman. In her fear-filled, confused state of mind, Cordee was fantasizing it would be her day of emancipation.

CHAPTER 19

Scratch a fantasy and you will find a nightmare.
—Gail Caldwell, *Let's Take the Long Way Home*

It was a day we all wish could be re-done. For reasons known only to her, Cordee drove to the county fair to visit her children who were working at a concession stand. They joined her on a carnival ride. Months later, in court, she remembered the morning as "a good day." It turned bad.

An evil urging guided Cordee as she arrived back at the house. The day was splendid, bright with mid-summer sunlight, but darkness had enveloped her. Cordee's eyes were locked in that all-too-familiar trance her doctors described as catatonic. What she truly felt one can only speculate. She was certainly mired in that uncertain wilderness of delusion, desperately attempting to sort out what was real and what was imagined. Reality included the twelve gauge shotgun resting in a closet just steps from where she stood. Fate rested on the direction her steps would take her next. She turned and made her way to where the gun and ammunition were stored. She surmised by evening she would be free to run away. Evening, however, was far off. The shotgun was near and she bent down, taking the lethal weapon into her quivering hands. She walked back to the kitchen.

Steve had already visited the Fleet Farm store on his way back from the Harley Davidson dealer in nearby Alexandria. He always ate a bag of popcorn while he walked the aisles looking for deals. Before he left for home, he picked up an extra bag for his kids. Steve was a good dad, his beloved children were always in his thoughts.

As Cordee made her way to the kitchen slowly, she was surprised by the strange beauty of the weapon. The varnished wood-grain stock was smooth to the touch. At this point the darkness descended on her and obscured any sane thoughts. The temporary insanity Cordee was experiencing juxtaposed the insanity of a society that made it far too easy for her to buy an inexpensive shotgun over the counter. Tragic as it is, even inexpensive shotguns have triggers, triggers strike firing pins, and firing pins ignite powder, sending projectiles into targets. At that moment, Cordee's intended target was mounting his motorcycle for the last time.

Cordee walked slowly and deliberately through the house and out the kitchen door to the sidewalk, which led to the gravel driveway. She released the lever on the shotgun. The barrel arched up and away from the trigger mechanism. Her shaking hands reached for the shell, which she carefully inserted into the barrel. After she snapped the barrel back in place she paused, pointed the shotgun to the sky, and fired the round. She stared into the cloudless sky for a few seconds, stunned by the force of the explosion. With a glacially slow movement she bent down, picked up the spent shell casing, turned, and made her way back toward the entry of the farmhouse. With a live round in her hand, she walked robotically into her house, unable to grasp the consequences of her intended actions. She sat down at the kitchen table and waited.

Upon hearing the deep-throated thump from the engine of Steve's Harley, she dropped the empty shell into the wastebasket and inserted a live round into the chamber of the shotgun. As Steve made his way up the sidewalk, Cordee carefully pulled the hammer into the firing position. He opened the kitchen door and sunlight filled the darkened room. He emerged wind-burned from his forty-mile bike ride. She thought he looked ruggedly handsome with his tanned face and sun-tinted hair. In another time with the kids out of the house, they might have made passionate love right there on the kitchen table. This, however, was a very different time. All she could envision was her husband kissing another woman, and it left her jealous and enraged. Upon entering the kitchen, Steve looked at Cordee and immediately glanced down at the shotgun. With a demanding and demeaning tone he said, "What's that?" Cordee responded coldly, "You know what it is." He walked slowly toward her and reached for the barrel of the shotgun. Cordee's finger twitched on the warm steel of the trigger. Her deliberate action forced the trigger to release the hammer, which came down with deadly precision upon the firing pin causing the powder to ignite, and sending the deadly charge out of the barrel. As the tumultuous relationship came to an end, Steve's eyes met Cordee's hollow stare for the last time. For an instant they locked in a gaze of surprise as the blast ripped into Steve's chest. He went down upon impact only to recover in a herculean manner, finding strength to stand and face his wife for the last time. His eyes went from registering quizzical surprise to an amazing expression of peace. Cordee saw he was looking up and beyond her. She found herself turning to see what was behind her. She then heard him fall to the floor. Turning back, she watched him collapse and realized that what he saw would elude her forever. Steve dropped to the kitchen floor. His body lay framed by the warm pool of deep-red blood pouring from his wound. His final move was to draw his arm across his face while exhaling a force of air that sounded like nothing Cordee had ever heard. Immediately the room went quiet, save the ringing in her ears and the sound of her husband's blood flowing from his body and pooling on the kitchen floor.

At that moment the only living being in the little house over-looking the Pelican River was Cordee Jo Tungseth. However, part of Cordee had died as well. For if loving compassion were truly alive within her she would have been moved to render aid, call for an ambulance, or to plead *I'm sorry*. Instead she calmly lit a cigarette and smoked it, the shotgun on the table and her dead husband lying prostrate on the floor.

When she had taken her last draw from the cigarette she ex-tinguished it, picked up the phone, and dialed 911. The dispatch officer answered the call and Cordee clearly spoke these words: "Steve Tungseth is dead. I just shot him." After hanging up the phone, she rose from her seat at the table and walked out into the searing July heat to wait.

CHAPTER 20

I aged rapidly during those months, as one must with such loss of one's self, with such proximity to death, and such distance from shelter.

  —Kay Jamison, *An Unquiet Mind*

I received the call from my father in the late afternoon on the Saturday Cordee killed Steve. My cell phone rang as I was returning from a horse show with my son. I nearly lost control of the three-quarter-ton Dodge Ram truck as my father's grief-stricken voice communicated the unfathomable news: "Matt, I need your help more than ever before. You need to take over for me right now. Cordee shot Steve. He is dead." I comforted my dad as best I could while attempting to keep calm enough as not to alarm my son. I needed more information before I shared with him the awful news about his beloved uncle and aunt. My goal for the moment was to protect my son who had been pulled out of the wreckage on a July evening the previous summer.

While my son listened to his iPod, I called a friend whom I knew had connections in law enforcement. I asked him to contact the Otter Tail County Sheriff's Office to get some details. My initial thought was Cordee and Steve had been in a fight. Steve had wielded a weapon and somehow in the struggle she had wrested control of the gun and fired. However, with Steve's tremendous strength I could not imagine how Cordee could manage such a feat. My friend's return call brought unimaginable news: "Matt," he said, "it's as bad as it gets. It appears she shot him intentionally. She killed him in cold blood."

When we arrived at the farm, Kathy and I gathered our dear son in our arms and shared with him the terrible news. We sat together on the steps of our log cabin. All we could do was weep.

Who could have imagined this? My two sisters' lives were ruined: one dead, another facing murder charges. Although I was surrounded by loving family and supported by dear friends, I did not know where to begin to pick up the pieces of a shattered family.

Questions haunted me so I learned all I could about bipolar disorder. I certainly was aware of the complexities that surround bipolar illness, but I struggled to understand how Cordee in a moment of blurred darkness pulled the trigger and murdered Steve. Those who suffer from bipolar disorder often do more harm to themselves than others. When killings occur, they are more often from an accidental act of manic madness rather than premeditated action. In fact, my sister Liz's accident and death serve as a case in point. Certainly it was an accident that claimed her life and nearly took the life of my son, but I believe the tragedy occurred as the result of a manic episode fueled by my father's prescription drugs. On the other hand Cordee clearly had a deeper psychological burden than Liz. I have learned since that she had yet another disorder, which contributed greatly to her actions leading up to the killing and how she responded after the fact. A few years after she was incarcerated as a result of her crime, Cordee had a breakdown, which caused her to be moved temporarily from the Minnesota Women's Correctional Facility at Shakopee to the state security hospital at St. Peter. The hospital at St. Peter provides evaluation and therapy for patients deemed by the courts to be mentally ill and dangerous. While the majority of the patients live out their days at St. Peter, it is also the only option the state has to treat prisoners from other institutions experiencing mental breakdowns while serving out their sentences. During her second stay in treatment for a deep paralyzing depression, the doctors discovered a condition previously undiagnosed. The discovery answered many of my questions. The doctors found she suffered from bipolar disorder and schizophrenia, which is a state known as schizoaffective disorder. On the day of Steve's death, Cordee was experiencing a number of the delusionary effects common to her then undiagnosed condition. So many things went wrong in the days, hours, and moments that led up to the dreadful consequence of Cordee's actions. Take away one of the delusions or situations she was experiencing on that day and this story may never have been written.

I wonder what would have happened if a friend or family member had called Cordee's cell phone as she waited at her kitchen table. What if one of the children would have returned home to pick up something they had forgotten? What if Steve would have kissed her as he left on his motorcycle ride? What if Cordee would have been taking her medication regularly, eating right, getting exercise, and connecting with concerned friends? What if Steve would have entered that kitchen with a warm smile, a gift or perhaps flowers? Finally, what if our father's dear friend would not have continued an adulterous relationship just to satisfy his selfish needs? As in Liz's story, there remain so many *what ifs* and *if onlys*. Alas, it was an unfathomable act caused by a horrible confluence of events and an unpredictable disease that resulted in an unimaginable outcome.

In the end, Steve Tungseth emerged as the one man who in Cordee's deranged mind represented all the men who had abused her and Liz throughout the years. Cordee created a new reality and vision for her future, fueled by an awful disease. Her bipolar episode and schizoaffective disorder ignited a number of delusional disorders including erotomatic (an incorrect belief that another person loved her), grandiose (an over-inflated perception of worth or power), jealous (believing her husband was unfaithful), and persecutory (the belief that she was about to be harmed). Her erotomanic disorder fed her fantasy of our father's friend being in love with her and waiting to whisk her away from her troubles. Her jealous disorder sent her into a spin thinking Steve would passionately kiss his former girlfriend while withholding kisses from Cordee. Her persecutory disorder caused her to believe Steve was going to harm her. It appears on that fateful day Cordee was exhibiting four of the five medically defined delusional disorders that comprise schizoaffective disorder. When an individual experiences two or more of these disorders it results in what the medical community labels "mixed disorder." Knowing she may have been experiencing this mix of disorders helps me understand the horrible outcomes of that July day. Perhaps she fantasized a kiss could melt away all the abuses she and her sister had endured. Those lifetime abuses included the hired man's actions, Steve's threat to kiss another woman, and all the myriad events of the forty years in between. In the end it was schizoaffective mental illness that opened the portal to the spiritual darkness which overtook Cordee's sweet soul and turned her, even if only for that one terrible moment, into a cold-blooded killer.

The morning after the killing I traveled to the Otter Tail County Jail to visit Cordee. Two of her children and a few of Steve's relatives were present; words were hard to come by. What could we say? In my private visit with Cordee we spoke, separated by glass. Although I am an ordained member of the clergy, as her brother I was treated with great suspicion and later learned that all of our conversations were recorded and used against her. I found Cordee to be in a robotic trance. Her first words were rather odd. "When will I be getting out? Have you come to get me?" I learned later her first words while entering the squad car after her arrest were: "Shall I pack a bag? Will I be spending the night or returning home before dark?" Later in that first visit she told me in a measured way that the reason she had killed Steve was because he had told her after an argument that he was going to kill her when he returned home. While this was not comforting to us as a family, it did for a time provide us a reason for why she had done such a thing. She later recanted the accusation.

In her delusion she actually believed once Steve was out of the way she would be safe and free to leave on holiday with her new boyfriend. She was imagining affection and adventure. In reality, the delusions would quickly fade as her twisted mind cleared. Her new-found clarity would reveal life would never be the same for her. Nor would it be for those who would be forced to navigate the wreckage her actions had caused.

CHAPTER 21

Now nearly all those I lived with and loved and did not under-stand when I was young are dead, but I still reach out to them.
— Norman McLain, *A River Runs Through It*

The fact remains it was Cordee and Cordee alone who picked up the shotgun, loaded it, and pulled the trigger to release the deadly charge. However, bipolar and schizoaffective disorders, along with a history of being abused emotionally, spiritually, and sexually, intensified her doubts and fears. At the deepest level our stories are alike. We all have desires, dreams, doubts, and fears, but it is different for those who struggle with diseased and unsettled minds. They must constantly battle their doubts and fears as they desperately seek to achieve normalcy and peace, dreams and desires.

Those of us who love Liz and Cordee feel victimized by the events their disease and life circumstances so ruthlessly visited upon us and others. During sleepless nights we cautiously ask ourselves if a dreaded disease has the power to wreak such havoc on the lives of our loved ones, are any of us safe? We ask this because the body of a beloved son, father, uncle, brother, and friend lies buried in a grave on the east edge of the Red River Valley.

We buried Steve as we gathered deep in grief, remembering the man who was and could have been. I stood off to the side feeling like an enemy because of my sister's crime, desperately wishing I could do or say something to ease the pain of my beloved nieces and nephews. I stood by, not only as an uncle and friend but also as a pastor, trained in the art of finding and speaking words of comfort, yet strangely devoid of anything that would help assuage their pain. I stepped back another pace and silently prayed.

As I write, eleven anniversaries of the burial have passed. Cordee served one year in Otter Tail County Jail, was convicted of murdering her husband, and was sentenced to serve her time in the Minnesota Correctional Institute for Women in Shakopee, Minnesota. She will be incarcerated until at least 2023, at which time she will be sixty-three years of age. The legal process presented an immediate challenge for my father and me. After her arrest, Cordee was charged with second-degree murder. Her bond was set at one million dollars. The court left open the possibility she could face a first-degree charge pending the outcome of a Grand Jury investigation. The first-degree murder charge carried with it the possibility of a life sentence. At her initial court appearance Cordee remained in a trance, her only response was to nod when the judge asked if she understood the charges. Her court-ordered attorney succeeded in getting the bail reduced to $250,000; nevertheless, she remained in custody. Our family, not understanding the situation, made the difficult decision to leave her in jail. We struggled mightily with this action, but made the decision with safety in mind. Cordee's case never went to trial. Ultimately, as a result of an agreement with the court, she pled guilty on the last day of February 2007 to second-degree murder in the shooting death of her husband on July 22, 2006. While the court acknowledged Cordee had struggled with mental health issues for twenty-six years, it found her case did not meet the standards for a mental health defense. She was sentenced to twenty-eight years in prison. Her attorney stated that "It was the just thing to do to give her the opportunity to get out of prison. Had she been found guilty of first-degree murder, the sentence would have been life without release. With good time and time served, she could be released in eighteen years and eight months from July 22, 2016."

On the day of her sentencing, Cordee, free of her previous trance, spoke. Much of the darkness had lifted. *The Fergus Falls Daily Journal* reported on her statement to the court.

> Speaking in a quiet, calm voice, Cordee Jo Tungseth apologized to family and friends for killing their father and brother and friend . . . "There's just no way to even begin to tell you how sorry I am . . . Sorry for the way I took him from you. I will live with that the rest of my life . . . There are just no words. I love you all very much. Thank you all for being here. Thank you for your support." [May 4, 2007]

Following the proceedings, she was transported to the Minnesota Correctional Facility for Women in Shakopee, Minnesota. Her attorney's final words to the court were as follows: "People don't ask for mental illness; it's there, but it is not their choice." Tungseth, he said, "has one hundred percent remorse, no question about it."

Our father, who loved and defended Liz and Cordee, died with a broken heart. He took comfort in the fact that while serving in the Minnesota State Legislature he was a tireless supporter of the state correctional system, never imagining one day his daughter would serve out a sentence in a facility he championed. Our mother died on a cold morning in January 2015. She lived her last years in a nursing home, her memory whittled down to events of long ago while absent of happenings in the very recent past. Her gravestone bears the message: "Oh how she loved us!"

Our sister Kit moved to Colorado during our mother's illness. Family members cope with tragedies differently. Kit chose to move out of state during our mother's last year and did not come back for the funeral. We have not spoken since, perhaps because we could never find the trust to share our deepest hurts. Some secrets go unrevealed, and they go with us to our graves. I guess I'll never know the true reason why she could not love me nor I her. Nevertheless, I will keep my promise to care and support Cordee as I did our parents.

A gift of grace from the Minnesota Correctional system involved giving Cordee the opportunity to see her mother and father before they died. On two separate occasions, about five years apart, Cordee was transported by guards to the nursing homes where our parents resided. With cuffed hands, she was afforded a half-hour visit, a chance to say goodbye. It was a time of love and healing, a profound gift for all involved.

Liz and Cordee's children have moved on and made lives of their own. Liz's three children and three of Cordee's four have visited the prison. The seven of them are bright, adventurous, and healthy. Cordee has two grandchildren, both of whom she has met and held. Liz did not live to see her two grandchildren. She would have loved being a grandma. Cordee and Liz's children understand the importance of support systems, and they work diligently to pursue those that promote healthful relationships, purging themselves of those that do not. They are survivors with sound minds and bodies. I love and respect them all as they seek to embrace all that was good about their mothers and leave behind that which was not. It is all any of us can do. I believe it is healthy to look back upon our childhoods to help us understand how we have developed into who we are. When mistakes are made we can learn from them and commit ourselves to do our best not to let history repeat itself. Conversely, it is important to recognize and name what was good and healthy and to seek to incorporate those traits into our relationships as we make our way in life. All of us will seek to put the puzzle pieces of our lives together. This quest may take a lifetime of honest searching, but there can be joy in the journey. In the end it is essential to extend a blessing of grace to those whom we lived with and loved, understood and misunderstood, through sickness and health.

I imagined I saw Steve one summer. It was the year we would have turned fifty-six together. But rather than seeing him in person, I had to settle for remembering what was and to dream about what might have been: I had to settle for something less than real because Steve is frozen in time, resting in the care of God. I had gone west to Montana to write and to make sense of all that had happened to my family. He came to me one day as a young father called to his kids in the Two Sisters café in Babb, Montana. Bothered by the noise, I looked up from my journal and saw a man of square jaw wearing a roughly-trimmed beard with wild windblown hair. His children climbed on him like puppies, clearly enjoying their father's attention. There was no mother present. I found it eerily strange that this remembrance of him would come to me as I was writing about the life my sister stole from him. In the young man, I received a glimpse of the wonderful yet firm father Steve had been. Memories of Steve flooded my mind. He had lived all of his life caught between a youthful disdain for organized religion and a deep traditional faith that he could not shake. Steve was a study in contradictions. He was generous yet stingy, freedom loving yet rigid. He lived according to his own rules, the same rules he rebelled against as a young man from a conservative Norwegian Lutheran pastor's family.

He ran to and away from church his entire life, while remaining steadfast in his personal faith. He loved his children dearly and tried in vain to love the two women who were his wives. He never came to understand those women, and since true love requires understanding, he found love painfully elusive. I imagine even Steve would admit that only two women fully understood and loved him. One was his mother, who kept him anchored to a fundamentally solid faith, and the other his first-born daughter, who embodied all that Steve valued and admired in women.

Steve's two wives tried without success to meet his ever changing and complicated needs. One bore him a son while the other gave him two daughters and two sons. His first wife, a high school sweetheart, fell in love with the rebel, but soon tired of competing for Steve's attention. She ended the marriage by signing a divorce decree and taking his son. His second wife, my sister Cordee, would also consider the pen as a weapon of choice but instead was driven to choose the twelve gauge shotgun to end the relationship permanently.

My anger nearly got the best of me that one day in the Mountains of Montana. I was ascending the Going to the Sun highway in Glacier National Park. I had finished my morning discipline of writing at the Two Sisters café; I was driving the pass mining my memory for images of my two sisters frolicking on our prairie farm forty-four years earlier. *If only*, I thought. If only Liz had not run away with the Texas playboy. If only he would not have sought primary custody of their children, an action that drove her to exhaustion on that fatal Fourth of July. If only . . .

Leaning into the snow-lined curves of Logan pass, I was pushing my wife's vintage Mazda Miata convertible to its limits. The squeal of the sliding tires reminded me of the family that had somehow spun out of control. I felt as though we were all part of the wreck and our family car was rolling down the mountain toward certain death. I was driving wickedly fast. I needed to stop before I destroyed my life. My tears flowed as I shouted questions at God.

I pulled the car to the side of the road. After opening the door, I got out and walked to a ledge that overlooked a thousand-foot vertical drop to the rocks below. "Enough!" I shouted to whatever evil was trying to destroy me. I needed to let go or jump. It was consuming my life. I thought and prayed for a long

time. I asked God to forgive me for all I had done and left undone, to lift the burden of guilt, and to help me understand all
that had happened.

CHAPTER 22

I went to the woods because I wished to live deliberately, to front only the essential facts of life, and see if I could not learn what it had to teach, and not, when I came to die, discover that I had not lived.

—Henry David Thoreau, *Walden*

The clouds that had hidden the majestic peaks of Glacier National Park began to lift. I stepped back from the ledge. It was a new day.

In my new-found clarity, I embraced our family's present and future realities. I had to let go of Steve, Cordee, and the devastation their conflict had brought upon us. Steve was dead, buried in sandy loam more than one thousand miles east of where I stood.

No, I did not see Steve in the Two Sisters café on that splendid summer morning. But I felt his spirit, just as I felt the spirits of my little sisters as they were before the ravages of disease and abuse changed them forever. My sister Liz either died screaming in terror or in the arms of a dear friend. I hope she breathed her last in the arms of her friend Gust. I am thankful he came upon the crash and pulled her from the wreck.

Steve would have died in terror if he hadn't summoned the strength to rise and look beyond the fixed eyes of the woman who shot him. After the blast Cordee looked behind and above to see what it was that changed his expression from confusion to one of peaceful repose. Whatever it was remains hidden from her. These days she spends her time walking endless corridors behind prison walls, seeking an elusive peace from behind locked doors.

I no longer write in my journal for hours seeking answers to my questions. I drove endless miles, read scores of books, asked hundreds of questions, and badgered God to reveal why it all happened like it did. My two yellow Labs, Pre and Kobuk, stood by faithfully and licked my cheeks as I cried my eyes out sitting in the big bluestem grass prairies of North Dakota. One day I set fire to the bunkhouse where the monster lived and tilled the ashes into the soil. I bulldozed and buried our family farmhouse and the dusty grain storage building. Peace and freedom from guilt emerged at last.

I know my children suffered as I pursued this endless quest to understand. Their constant and unconditional love sustained me on the journey. I love them for walking with me through my despair. They cried with me, laughed with me, and skied with me on water and snow. Together with their mom we rode horses, galloping at full speed across family land we all care for dearly.

My search for understanding and peace took me over thousands of miles, to some of the most beautiful places in this country. But my heart always led me home to the prairie. True peace for me came in the presence, essence, and love of the woman who was always there to meet me at the door of the log cabin we built together in 1980. She is the woman I fell in love with the very first time our eyes met, bringing color to a black and white world, grace in the midst of law, and joy in a world of sorrow. She is the woman whom I love and understand and who loves, understands, and kisses me with passion and tenderness. Together we buried our first born baby girl in our farmyard after she died in her crib from Sudden Infant Death Syndrome. We stayed on the farm and raised three amazing children. The certainty of her love trumps any questions that return to haunt me.

Papa and Mom on their honeymoon in Sun Valley Idaho. Matt would come along seven months later.

Our beautiful mother in the summer of 1956

Kit and Allen in 1978

Cordee as Moorhead High School Homecoming Queen. Her response to the crowd after being crowned: "We're all just dust and my dust isn't any better than your dust."

Liz and Cordee running free in the summer of 1978

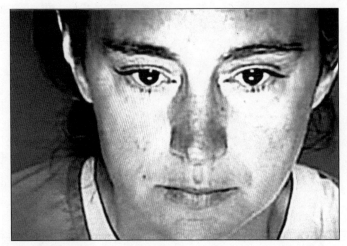

Cordee on the day of her arrest

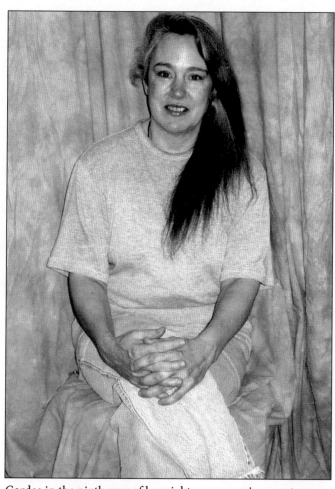

Cordee in the ninth year of her eighteen-year prison sentence

Matt visiting Cordee in 2017 at Shakopee Women's Correctional Facility

AFTERWORD

Here in the world beautiful and terrible things will happen. Don't be afraid.
　　　　　—Fredrik Buechner, *Beyond Words*

Amazingly, Cordee and Liz's children have moved on in their own ways. Most days and seasons find them thriving. All the members of the families caught in the twisted mania told in my story had to let something go in order to move beyond the accumulated anger and shame we felt. As anger and shame co-conspired with grief and loss, it became increasingly difficult to sort out what had been left behind and what needed to remain. Before we can move on we must live through a dark night to see another day. Every day the fight for redemption and reconciliation goes toe to toe with our natural inclination toward blame and retribution. Moving on is about honestly naming this fight.

Another inescapable fact is that life goes on. For the survivor, for the living, any other option is unacceptable. For my sister Cordee, she is blessed to be a sister, a mother, a grandmother, and a friend. These connections and relationships are challenging and complicated. However, those of us who are in relationships with Cordee are of the Christian faith, and we are called to love one another no matter what. A remarkable core group of people have been able to do so, and as a result have become essential elements in Cordee's road to redemption and health. They continue to visit her, support her, and pray for her. They have been there time and time again for her and Steve's children. They are examples of amazing grace.

As for me, I continue to struggle with my anger for the men who hurt my sisters and the disease that impacted their otherwise promising lives. However, an evolving miracle that has helped me to cope has been the rediscovery of my love for Cordee beyond the wreckage of her horrible act. The process that allowed this rediscovery involved cultivating an understanding of the disease and the circumstances which led to her actions on July 22, 2006. My love and respect for Cordee grows deeper as we have talked honestly about the horrible struggles she has endured. Prison has helped restore her health, as she receives excellent health care along with consistent emotional and spiritual support. The warden knows her by name as does the chaplain whom she often assists at weekly worship. In my community support work I have come across individuals who have served time in prison. On two occasions I asked if they knew my sister Cordee and in each case their eyes lit up. One of them commented in an astonished tone: "Your sister is Cordee! We call her the kind murder lady. At first we were scared of her because we had heard what she had done to her husband. But that all changed as we came to know her. She prays for us, she is kind and gentle. You have a wonderful sister." Once, at the beginning of her prison sentence, Cordee was deep in despair and crying throughout my visit with her. The only advice I could give her was to tell her she would just have to make a meaningful life out of the years she was sentenced to serve. She looked at me and said: "With your help and prayers I promise to try." She has kept that promise, and in her own way she has made a life.

I would go so far to say she has not only made a life but also a ministry, a calling, if you will.

In June of 2017, after visiting Cordee, I was getting into my car when I heard someone calling, "Hey, Uncle Matt!" Looking across the parking lot I was delighted to see one of Cordee's twin sons. He was with his lovely wife, and in his arms was their three-month-old son. They were on their way to visit Cordee; it would be the first time she got a chance to hold her only grandson. The little family of three was happy, healthy, and making a life of their own while at the same time honoring Cordee with a visit.

The next day Cordee called me. She was ecstatic as she shared how wonderful it was to see her son happily married and with a family of his own. Their visit gave her new-found hope. She went on to say she had passed the halfway point of her sentence, with release then only eight years away. She imagines being free with an eight-year-old grandson and a ten-year-old grand-daughter to love on the outside. She shared her grief for a son and daughter who are still estranged from her. I jokingly remind her a baseball player who bats .500 is unheard of. She laughs with me and then we share tears as well. Tears of what was and what is and what will be.

We will remember those whom we have loved and lost. We will remain thankful for what was and dream of what might have been. We will ask God to bless the good memories and heal the painful ones. We will cling to hope and love, because in the end hope and love are all we have.

While this is a story of the secrets my sisters endured, it is also a story of my revealing those secrets and what the telling has revealed in me. Perhaps it is also a reminder of secrets that remain in all of us. Secrets which, if not shared, will go with us to our graves, impacting our behavior until we breathe our last breath. Although I was not visited with the disease my sisters shared, I endured my share of grief and abuse. What was different? Why did I survive the darkness and hopelessness I encountered along the way? Will I survive the inevitable crises, which I know await me, the secrets yet unrevealed? I hope so; however, as this story reveals, life is not predictable or fair.

Often, at the end of day, I spend time at the grave of our first-born daughter, Katie Anne. She died on a cold morning in 1982 on the thirteenth of February. Our first Valentine's Day card to her remains unopened after all these years. One never fully recovers from losing a daughter before her first birthday. On some nights I am haunted with the memory of running from our bedroom in response to my wife's urgent scream from the nursery. She is holding the stiffening body of our dear Katie Anne. My thoughts turn into a dreamlike tangle of cries, prayers, calls, sirens, CPR, a hospital emergency room, and our distraught doctor reaching out to hug us. It's not always like this; on other nights I imagine seeing Katie again. She is safe, warm, and beautiful. The swirling images from the nursery, hospital, funeral home, and graveside subside, and I imagine her happy and at peace. On one profound night she came to me through a dream: *Don't worry Papa, and please don't be angry at God. If you must be angry, be angry at death. It was death that stole me from you and Mom. I know you were terrified and hurting, but God was there right away. God took me from death. I'm okay. Really I am.*

On cold, dark, late winter afternoons when I stand outside immersed in memories, I look west to the century-old cottonwood trees that anchor our farmstead. They remain frozen in deep winter's grasp, dark as ebony against the fading horizon. Yet, moments before the sun leaves, it sends a glorious array of splendid colors skyward in a gallant attempt to ward off the coming night. Even as the day succumbs to the impending darkness, the signal is clear that the fight in the light remains. On some nights, I walk with my wife to our little barn to feed our horses and dogs. Even on the darkest evenings, the night sky illuminates the Ponderosa pines we planted along the lane when our love was new. The now towering trees guide the way. As we continue on the worn path, our love of more than forty years warms us, and our faith in the Creator sustains us. With our chores done, we step into the warmth of the cabin, aware of tomorrow's uncertainties yet grateful for the opportunity to move on.

ABOUT THE AUTHOR

The Reverend Matthew Valan lives with his wife of forty-one years on the home quarter of the Red River Valley family farm his paternal grandfather founded in 1903. Valan earned his BA in Political Science and History from Concordia College in Moorhead, Minnesota, and holds a Master of Divinity Degree from Luther Seminary in St. Paul, Minnesota. His entire career of thirty-six years in youth and family ministry has taken place in the Fargo–Moorhead (North Dakota and Minnesota) community. He is a nationally recognized speaker on youth, family, and educational issues. Valan serves on the Board of Moorhead Area Public Schools and is active in many community organizations. He is currently senior pastor of Messiah Lutheran Church in Fargo and preaching pastor of The Hour of Worship television ministry reaching parts of a four-state area as well as southern portions of Manitoba and Saskatchewan. Valan and his family are in the second year of a native prairie restoration project on their "back forty" called Dreamfields. Together with his wife, children, and grandchildren he rides horses, skis on water and snow, and hunts with his three dogs: Pre, Kaizer, and Doc. Valan loves to read and write in the log cabin he and his wife built with friends on the farm in 1980. A cancer and abuse survivor, he now lives each day with a spirit of gratitude.

ABOUT THE PRESS

North Dakota State University Press (NDSU Press) exists to stimulate and coordinate interdisciplinary regional scholarship. These regions include the Red River Valley, the state of North Dakota, the plains of North America (comprising both the Great Plains of the United States and the prairies of Canada), and comparable regions of other continents. We publish peer reviewed regional scholarship shaped by national and international events and comparative studies.

Neither topic nor discipline limits the scope of NDSU Press publications. We consider manuscripts in any field of learning. We define our scope, however, by a regional focus in accord with the press's mission. Generally, works published by NDSU Press address regional life directly, as the subject of study. Such works contribute to scholarly knowledge of region (that is, discovery of new knowledge) or to public consciousness of region (that is, dissemination of information, or interpretation of regional experience). Where regions abroad are treated, either for comparison or because of ties to those North American regions of primary concern to the press, the linkages are made plain. For nearly three-quarters of a century, NDSU Press has published substantial trade books, but the line of publications is not limited to that genre. We also publish textbooks (at any level), reference books, anthologies, reprints, papers, proceedings, and monographs. The press also considers works of poetry or fiction, provided they are established regional classics or they promise to assume landmark or reference status for the region. We select biographical or autobiographical works carefully for their prospective contribution to regional knowledge and culture. All publications, in whatever genre, are of such quality and substance as to embellish the imprint of NDSU Press.

We changed our imprint to North Dakota State University Press in January 2016. Prior to that, and since 1950, we published as the North Dakota Institute for Regional Studies Press. We continue to operate under the umbrella of the North Dakota Institute for Regional Studies, located at North Dakota State University.